FACING
A TASK
UNFINISHED

Our Lord Jesus did not say, 'You shall do witnessing.' He said, 'You shall be my witnesses' (Acts 1:8). Implications of this difference are profound and far reaching in that evangelism is not limited to a few who have the 'gift'; it is, rather, the privilege of everyone whose life is grounded in Christ. Emerging from this conviction, Roger Carswell presents the heart, soul, and practical routines of gospel witness.

Chris Castaldo,
Lead Pastor, New Covenant Church, Naperville, Illinois
and Author of *Talking with Catholics about the Gospel*

Week 49 – Matthew 18 verses 1 to 5

Roger writes, "Sadly around us are children for whom nobody prays ... today you could start praying for an un-prayed for child."

With these words, Roger Carswell sent me to my sons' playground with a whole new vision. I'm sure some of the children there have never been prayed for before and it's been wonderful to feel I'm the first person to pray for them. This book is a great encouragement and stimulation to evangelism, written by a man, who has worked tirelessly for the gospel for decades. It's been great to see what has kept him going.

Rico Tice
Author, Christianity Explored &
Senior Minister for Evangelism, All Souls Church, Langham
Place, London

FACING
A TASK
UNFINISHED

Cultivating Personal Evangelism Week by Week

Roger Carswell

TRUTHFOR**LIFE**®

CHRISTIAN
FOCUS

Copyright © Roger Carswell 2011
paperback ISBN: 978-1-78191-581-3
epub ISBN: 978-1-78191-615-5
mobi ISBN: 978-1-78191-616-2

First published in 2011
ISBN: 978-1-84550-730-5

This edition published in 2015
Reprinted in 2020
by
Christian Focus Publications,
Geanies House, Fearn,
Ross-shire, IV20 1TW, Scotland, UK
www.christianfocus.com
and
Truth For Life
P.O. Box 398000 Cleveland
Ohio 44139, USA

Cover design by Daniel van Straaten

Printed in the USA

CONTENTS

Introduction

The fact that you have got hold of this devotional book is probably an indication that you are concerned, even burdened, that people should come to know the Lord Jesus. We long for the Lord to be honoured and His name glorified on earth. We want people to find forgiveness and new life through the finished work of Jesus on the cross. We pray that the Holy Spirit would work in their hearts to convict and convert them.

Ever since my conversion to Christ, through the faithful witness of my family and relatives, I have had an overwhelming desire for people to come to faith in Christ, and then for those who are His to be involved in the great work of soul-winning and disciple-making. I thank God that for many Christians today, evangelism has gone high on the agenda of both the joys and responsibilities of Christian living. Longing for the Lord to be glorified, aware of the Great Commission, concerned about the decline in church attendance, burdened about how very lost are the people we meet and encouraged by a number of evangelistic aids, we have increasingly prayed for those around us.

For some, the daily 'quiet time' — that discipline whereby a time is set aside each day as a key part of our walk with God, to read the Bible, pray and even sing — has become rather passé. But for others there is no substitute for those valuable minutes which set the tone for the day ahead. They are like tuning the guitar before playing, or limbering up before jogging, or putting on protective clothing before going into battle.

Time and again, in wanting to be regular in praying for the work and workers in God's kingdom, I have compiled a list of those for whom I will be praying regularly. It helps in remembering, as well as in being disciplined and faithful.

This little book seeks to combine Christian hymns and songs which have a soul-winning theme, with relevant passages from the Bible and ideas for prayer, which express our desire to see others coming to saving faith in Jesus Christ. If the hymns are known you may wish to sing them quietly, but otherwise they can be read prayerfully as part of the meditation. My prayer is that this book might become a tool to help us keep focused on prayerfully seeing each new day as one where we can live and speak for the Lord Jesus.

I can imagine that for many people the hymns I have used will be unfamiliar. I love many of the new hymns that we are singing as congregations, and have trawled over the more modern hymns with which I am familiar, but have had little success in finding any with an individual's soul-winners' passion. Perhaps this is a sad reflection on the Christian community which has omitted concern for the lost in our singing recently. I would be thrilled if this book was a catalyst for some modern song writers to include evangelism in their inventory of hymn themes.

I am also aware that some of the lyrics appear sentimental or 'cringe-worthy', but I have included them deliberately to remind ourselves of the very great need to have genuine concern for people in their various needs. 'Be kind; you do not know what battles people are fighting' is good advice, and what may appear over-emotional to us may be in tune with the deep emotions someone longs to express to the Lord and others. For remember, many of the hymns are, in themselves, prayers.

May I wholeheartedly thank Mrs Jean Smith of Leicester, Mr Os Ross of Long Crendon, and my son Ben working with Tertiary Students' Christian Fellowship in New Zealand, for their many helpful and constructive comments. The improvements that they made are many, though any weaknesses still remaining are entirely mine.

How to use this book

I think most of us find it easier to begin a project than to complete it. The great missionary pioneer, James Hudson Taylor, said, 'A man or woman may be dedicated and devoted, but if ill-disciplined will be useless.' This little book is not intended to be an easy read, but an aid to devotion to help us focus on the heart of the Lord who takes no pleasure in the death of the wicked, and desires that all people should be saved. The book is not meant to be gruelling or irksome. One old saint reflected, 'My greatest delight in life is to be in a nook with *the* Book.' Of course as we consider the plight of people outside of Christ, there will be challenge, but if that leads us more to become like Jesus, then we know that there will be blessings in store for us.

I recommend setting aside time each day when, without the distractions of anything else, you spend time with God. If you can find a quiet place, all the better. I find it helpful to quietly sing a hymn to tune my heart to praise God, then to pray and read the Bible.[1] In praying we speak with God, and in reading the Bible we are opening the lips of God and allowing Him to speak to us. 'Facing a Task Unfinished' is intended to be used in addition to our daily quiet time.

Maybe it could be used on Sunday afternoons, or perhaps at a set time on one particular evening each week, but over the course of a year it should help you to spend a few extra minutes meditating and praying, particularly about the needs of the world around us. If you miss, don't be discouraged or give up, but go back to where you last were and continue.

It would be ideal if you were following *Facing a Task Unfinished* at the same pace as someone else, so you could keep each other up to date on the plan. Maybe a small group in your church, or all the church, could corporately follow the plan. It is not an end in itself. Its great end is the glory of God.

At the end of the book are pages for you to write lists of people and events for which you want to regularly pray. Below is a suggestion, but it is from my 'Prayer Book', and you will want to arrange the days to suit what is best for your life.

---

1. I wholeheartedly recommend *Search the Scriptures*, published by IVP, as the best guide to get to grips with what the Bible is teaching. It takes three years to complete, but will enable you to really study the Bible in depth. Alternatively, *More Precious than Gold*, one of the Didasko file booklets explains about the quiet time, and includes the Bible reading scheme of Robert Murray McCheyne, a nineteenth-century Scottish minister who was greatly used by the Lord. It is a demanding, but greatly rewarding system for reading the Bible through in a year, and the New Testament through twice in the year. They are both available from your local Christian bookshop, or at discounted price from www.10ofthose.com

Finally, let me testify to the immense blessing that a particular hymn has been to me. I have only seen it published in the Young Life[2] Hymnal. It is like a battle hymn for all who are evangelising. It was taught to me and regularly sung in the inter-church meetings and missions I attended as a young Christian. I find it deeply challenging, and in many ways it has been the music behind the flickering passion I have for people to come to Christ. Countless times I have used its words in my devotions, and I share it with you in the hope that it might grip your heart as it has mine.

With a soul blood-bought and a heart aglow,
Redeemed of the Lord and free,
I ask as I pass down the busy street,
Is it only a crowd I see?
Do I lift my eyes with a careless gaze,
That pierces no deep-down woe,
Have I naught to give to the teeming throng
Of the wealth of the love I know?

Let me look at the crowd as my Saviour did,
Till my eyes with tears grow dim;
Let me look till I pity the wandering sheep,
And love them for love of Him.

As I read in the gospel story oft
Of the Christ who this earth once trod,
I fancy I see His look on the crowd,
That look of the Son of God;
He saw not a number in might and strength,
But a shepherdless flock distressed

---

2. Formerly known as the National Young Life Campaign.

And the sight of those wearied fainting sheep
Brought grief to His loving breast.

Dear Lord, I ask for the eyes that see,
Deep down to the world's sore need,
I ask for a love that holds not back,
But pours out itself indeed;
I want the passionate power of prayer,
That yearns for the great crowd's soul,
I want to go among the fainting sheep
And tell them my Lord makes whole.

— Mrs R. A. Jarvie

The Heart of
the Gospel

Week 1

1 Corinthians 1:17–2:2 (NLT)

F or Christ didn't send me to baptise, but to preach the Good News — and not with clever speech, for fear that the cross of Christ would lose its power. The message of the cross is foolish to those who are headed for destruction! But we who are being saved know it is the very power of God. As the Scriptures say,

> *'I will destroy the wisdom of the wise and discard the intelligence of the intelligent.'*

So where does this leave the philosophers, the scholars, and the world's brilliant debaters? God has made the wisdom of this world look foolish. Since God in His wisdom saw to it that the world would never know Him through human wisdom, He has used our foolish preaching to save those who believe. It is foolish to the Jews, who ask for signs from heaven and it is foolish to the Greeks, who seek human wisdom. So when we preach that Christ was crucified, the Jews are offended and the Gentiles say 'it's all nonsense'.

But to those called by God to salvation, both Jews and Gentiles, Christ is the power of God and the wisdom of God. This foolish plan of God is wiser than the wisest of human plans, and God's weakness is stronger than the greatest of human strength.

Remember, dear brothers and sisters, that few of you were wise in the world's eyes or powerful or wealthy when God called you. Instead, God chose things the world considers foolish in order to shame those who think they are wise. And He chose things that are powerless to shame those who are powerful. God chose things despised by the world, things counted as nothing at all, and used them to bring to nothing what the world considers important. As a result, no one can ever boast in the presence of God.

God has united you with Christ Jesus. For our benefit God made Him to be wisdom itself. Christ made us right with God; He made us pure and holy, and He freed us from sin. Therefore, as the Scriptures say, 'If you want to boast, boast only about the Lord.'

When I first came to you, dear brothers and sisters, I didn't use lofty words and impressive wisdom to tell you God's secret plan. For I decided that while I was with you I would forget everything except Jesus Christ, the one who was crucified.

Meditation

At the Keswick Convention in the year 2000, Rev. John Stott outlined this passage by saying it is about:

1. The weakness of the evangel (i.e. the gospel message);

2. The weakness of the evangelised;

3. The weakness of the evangelist.

That is exactly what the Apostle Paul is teaching, and though the gospel is hardly macho, it is 'Christ and Him crucified' which is the good news that we have to share with our world. As witnesses to the truth of Jesus, we are not Old Testament prophets called to denounce the sins of the nations, but Christians who are wanting the world to know of Jesus 'the Friend of sinners'. Non-believers are not our enemies; they are as we once were, and we want them to be as we are now.

We have a gospel to proclaim,
Good news for men in all the earth,
The gospel of a Saviour's name:
We sing His glory, tell His worth.

Tell of His birth at Bethlehem,
Not in a royal house or hall
But in a stable dark and dim:
The Word made flesh, a light for all.

Tell of His death at Calvary,
Hated by those He came to save;
In lonely suffering on the cross
For all He loved, His life He gave.

Tell of that glorious Easter morn:
Empty the tomb, for He was free;
He broke the power of death and hell
That we might share His victory.

Tell of His reign at God's right hand,
By all creation glorified;
He sends His Spirit on His Church
To live for Him, the Lamb who died.

Now we rejoice to name Him King —
Jesus is Lord of all the earth;

This gospel message we proclaim,
We sing His glory, tell His worth.
— EDWARD J. BURNS

Prayer

Gracious Heavenly Father, as I begin working through this little book, first help me to be diligent in following it right through. Then, please help me to grow in having a Christ-like attitude to the people on every continent, in every country, of every culture and whatever colour of skin. May I see them as people whom You have made and love, and for whom Christ died. May I love them for Jesus' sake. Amen.

My personal prayer:

....

....

....

....

....

....

Week 2

T *he grace of our Lord Jesus Christ be with you all.*
Amen. Now to Him who is able to establish you
according to my gospel and the preaching of Jesus Christ,
according to the revelation of the mystery kept secret
since the world began but now made manifest, and by
the prophetic Scriptures made known to all nations,
according to the commandment of the everlasting God,
for obedience to the faith—to God, alone wise, be glory
through Jesus Christ forever. Amen.

Meditation

It was a pattern of the Apostle Paul to open or close a
letter which he was writing by praying a prayer that
summarized the burden of the letter. This is what he
is doing here at the end of his letter to the Romans.
Paul had not yet visited the church at Rome, so he
uses the letter to clearly spell out exactly what the
gospel is all about. He did not take it for granted that
the professing Christians of Rome clearly understood how the Christ who had been anticipated for
centuries had now appeared and accomplished in

His death, redemption and reconciliation to God for all who believe, both Jew and Gentile. There is still today value and blessing for those who will take time to explain the gospel to people who, though religious, have not understood the inclusiveness of the gospel of grace to all who will repent and believe.

I cannot speak a proper word,
Nor think aright, but from the Lord
Preparing heart and tongue;
In nature I can see no good,
But all my good proceeds from God,
And does to grace belong.

I see it now, and do confess
My utter need of Jesus' grace,
And of His Spirit's light;
I beg His kind and daily care;
O Lord, my heart and tongue prepare
To think and speak aright.

Prepare my tongue to pray and praise,
To speak of providential ways,
And heavenly truth unfold;
To strengthen well a feeble soul,
Correct the wanton, rouse the dull,
And silence sinners bold.

— JOHN BERRIDGE

Prayer

O God of the gospel, may I never be ashamed of who You are, and what You have done. I rejoice that in all areas of this earth are those who are

Yours through the grace of the Lord Jesus Christ. Thank you that people of all nationalities and backgrounds as well as of different economic and social status, young and old, male and female are one in Christ. May I be a winsome busybody enquiring about the spiritual state of those whom I know, and helping to establish them in the gospel of Jesus Christ, in whose name I pray, Amen.

My personal prayer:

....

....

....

....

....

....

Week 3

Galatians 3:1-4

O foolish Galatians! Who has bewitched you that you should not obey the truth, before whose eyes Jesus Christ was clearly portrayed among you as crucified? This only I want to learn from you: Did you receive the Spirit by the works of the law, or by the hearing of faith? Are you so foolish? Having begun in the Spirit, are you now being made perfect by the flesh? Have you suffered so many things in vain—if indeed it was in vain?

Meditation

The people who heard Paul preach in Galatia, who were then converted, didn't physically see Jesus crucified. So when Paul writes 'before whose eyes Jesus Christ was clearly portrayed among you as crucified', he is reminding them of the messages they heard from Paul himself. Paul preached in such a way that he turned people's ears into eyes and they saw the truth. People's minds are picture galleries more than debating chambers, but in portraying truth with words, we must make sure that we are making much of Christ and Him crucified. It is when people 'see' Christ on the cross that they are drawn to Him. Having been lifted up on the cross, He draws people to Him. Human pride is such that we try to make our own deeds part of the process by which we are saved. Scripture, time and again, warns us against this. Christ, and He alone, saves people.

How sweet the name of Jesus sounds
In a believer's ear!
It soothes his sorrows, heals his wounds,
And drives away his fear.

It makes the wounded spirit whole,
And calms the troubled breast;
'Tis manna to the hungry soul,
And to the weary, rest.

Dear name, the rock on which I build,
My shield and hiding place,
My never-failing treasury, filled
With boundless stores of grace!

Jesus! My Shepherd, Saviour, Friend,
My Prophet, Priest and King,
My Lord, my Life, my Way, my End,
Accept the praise I bring.

Weak is the effort of my heart,
And cold my warmest thought;
But when I see Thee as Thou art,
I'll praise Thee as I ought.

Till then I would Thy love proclaim
With every fleeting breath;
And may the music of Thy name
Refresh my soul in death.

— JOHN NEWTON

Prayer

I praise You Heavenly Father, for all that Jesus accomplished in those three days' work, where He was crucified, buried and raised from the dead. Help me, as I go into each new day, to so speak of the Lord Jesus that people may see Him with the eye of faith, and turning from their sin, trust Him as Lord and Saviour. May Jesus be my passion, my desire, my love, my reason for speaking and my focus in witnessing. I pray for His glory alone. Amen.

My personal prayer:

....

....

....

....

....

....

Week 4
Genesis 12:1-3

*N*ow the L*ord* had said to Abram: 'Get out of your country, from your family and from your father's house, to a land that I will show you. I will make you a great nation; I will bless you and make your name great; and you shall be a blessing. I will bless those who bless you, and I will curse him who curses you; and in you all the families of the earth shall be blessed.'

Isaiah 52:13-15

*B*ehold, My Servant shall deal prudently; He shall be exalted and extolled and be very high. Just as many were astonished at you,* so His visage was marred more than any man, and His form more than the sons of men; so shall He sprinkle many nations. Kings shall shut their mouths at Him; for what had not been told them they shall see, and what they had not heard they shall consider.
*Some versions read 'Him'.

Meditation

Only Jesus had His biography written before He was born. For centuries, faithful men and women looked forward to His coming. They knew how He would be born and where. There were prophecies concerning His life and ministry. They were even told the details and significance of His death and everlasting role. They looked forward to His coming; we look back and rejoice as did Abraham to 'see His day'. We have seen all nations being blessed by Jesus and long to see that prophecy increasingly being fulfilled. The blood of Jesus is sufficient to sprinkle all nations, to silence kings and stun those who hear the gospel for the first time. And yet we must be aware, as Martin Luther expressed it, 'the world is bitterly opposed to the Ten Commandments, [so the fact] that it lies and deceives, steals, robs and murders, is not strange.'

❦

Great God of Abraham! hear our prayer
Let Abraham's seed Thy mercy share;
Oh, may they now at length return,
And look on Him they pierced, and mourn.

Remember Jacob's flock of old;
Bring home the wanderers to Thy fold;
Remember too Thy promised word,
'Israel at last shall seek the Lord.'

Though outcasts still, estranged from Thee,
Cut off from their own olive tree;
Why should they longer such remain?
For Thou canst graft them in again.

Lord, put Thy law within their hearts,
And write it in their inward parts;

The veil of darkness rend in two,
Which hides Messiah from their view.

Oh! haste the day, foretold so long,
When Jew and Greek, a glorious throng,
One house shall seek, one prayer shall pour,
And one Redeemer shall adore!

— THOMAS COTTERILL

Prayer

Thank you, dear God, that heaven is populated by men and women who are each there because of Jesus. Some looked forward to His coming; I look back 2,000 years to Him. Thank you that He is the same yesterday, today and forever. Thank you that heaven is not a reward, but a gift of grace. Continue to gather in a people whose sole dependence is upon You, that Your people will be complete in Christ and a complete family in Heaven. Thank you for assuring me in Your Word of answering this prayer. In the name of Jesus. Amen.

My personal prayer:

....

....

....

....

....

....

The Gospel to All Nations

Week 5

Luke 24:13-16, 44-49

*N*ow behold, two of them were travelling that same day to a village called Emmaus, which was seven miles from Jerusalem. And they talked together of all these things which had happened. So it was, while they conversed and reasoned, that Jesus Himself drew near and went with them. But their eyes were restrained, so that they did not know Him.

... Then He said to them, 'These are the words which I spoke to you while I was still with you, that all things must be fulfilled which were written in the Law of Moses and the Prophets and the Psalms concerning Me.' And He opened their understanding, that they might comprehend the Scriptures. Then He said to them, 'Thus it is written, and thus it was necessary for the Christ to suffer and to rise from the dead the third day, and that repentance and remission of sins should be preached in His name to all nations, beginning at Jerusalem. And you are witnesses of these things. Behold, I send the Promise of My Father upon you; but tarry in the city of Jerusalem until you are endued with power from on high.'

Meditation

What a delightful snapshot of Jesus the Pastor, the Wonderful Counsellor drawing alongside the downcast, doubting disciples as they walked and talked about Jesus. Throughout His life this is what Jesus did, drew alongside the doubting, the despondent, the grieving, the sick, the lonely, the struggling and even the dying. Here Jesus used the Word to point the two disciples to Himself and the gospel itself, insisting that the Christ had to suffer, die and the third day rise again. What a Bible study that must have been, and what a role model is Jesus. To effectively cure the hearts of lost men and women, we need the best tool, which is the Bible, and time, and talk! Much good conversation about Jesus comes about when we have the time to start at the beginning and carefully tell people of Jesus. It is a good thing to always have a Bible, and be ready to open it and explain who is the Person to whom it all points. Isn't this what life is actually about? Sir Wilfred Grenfell said, 'The service we render for others is really the rent we pay for our room on this earth.'

How shall they hear the Word of God
Unless His truth is told?
How shall the sinful be set free,
The sorrowful consoled?
To all who speak the truth today
Impart your Spirit, Lord we pray.

How shall they call to God for help
Unless they have believed?

How shall the poor be given hope,
The prisoner reprieved?
To those who help the blind to see
Give light and love and clarity.

How shall the gospel be proclaimed
If heralds are not sent?
How shall the world find peace at last
If we are negligent?
So send us, Lord, for we rejoice
To speak of Christ with life and voice.

— © Michael Perry

Prayer

Lord of all, I confess that so often I am just too busy to stop and talk to people about Jesus. Please forgive me. Impress upon me that the greatest investment of my life is to point people to Jesus. Guide me by your Holy Spirit to draw alongside the hurting and those with hearts that are ready to hear the good news that Christ had to suffer and rise, so that we might experience His forgiveness. May I be a faithful, fruitful witness to Your grace and goodness. I pray in Jesus' name. Amen.

My personal prayer:

....

....

....

....

....

....

Week 6

Joshua 6:20-25 (NLT)

The Fall of Jericho

*W*hen *the people heard the sound of the rams' horns, they shouted as loud as they could. Suddenly, the walls of Jericho collapsed, and the Israelites charged straight into the town and captured it. They completely destroyed everything in it with their swords—men and women, young and old, cattle, sheep, goats, and donkeys.*

Meanwhile, Joshua said to the two spies, 'Keep your promise. Go to the prostitute's house and bring her out, along with all her family.'

The men who had been spies went in and brought out Rahab, her father, mother, brothers, and all the other relatives who were with her. They moved her whole family to a safe place near the camp of Israel.

Then the Israelites burned the town and everything in it. Only the things made from silver, gold, bronze, or iron were kept for the treasury of the LORD's house. So Joshua spared Rahab the prostitute and her relatives who were with her in the house, because she had hidden the spies Joshua sent to Jericho. And she lives among the Israelites to this day.

Meditation

Rahab, the prostitute of Jericho, in an act of faith, had given refuge to the two spies sent by Joshua to spy out the land. They had been a blessing to her, and then promised that if she bound a scarlet cord in the window, through which they had escaped, everyone who was within her house would be saved. About three weeks passed before the Israelite army marched around the walls of Jericho. However, on the seventh day they marched around the city seven times. The walls fell down and the city was routed.

The young men, who had been spies, went to Rahab's house and brought out Rahab, her father, mother, brothers and 'all that she had'. That phrase is written in 6:23 and 25. Clearly she had spent her time with her family, friends and anyone else she knew, earnestly and urgently persuading them to come to the place of safety. Little did she realise how vital that task would be to so many. It was her greatest act of love.

Even more, she was to be an ancestor of Jesus. Her self-sacrificing led to immediate and long term blessing to millions because of what her greater Son would accomplish. Is God not able to use us to bless those around us, and maybe bring the Saviour to generations yet to come if we will spend time with those we would aim to win to Christ? David Siegmann said, 'God is in the people-saving business, and His method is to use His people.'

Church of God, elect and glorious,
Holy nation, chosen race;
Called as God's own special people,
Royal priests and heirs of grace;
Know the purpose of your calling,
Show to all His mighty deeds;
Tell of love which knows no limits,
Grace which meets all human needs.

God has called you out of darkness
Into His most marvellous light;
Brought His truth to light within you,
Turned your blindness into sight.
Let your light so shine around you
That God's name is glorified;
And all find fresh hope and purpose
In Christ Jesus crucified.

Once you were an alien people,
Strangers to God's heart of love;
But He brought you home in mercy,
Citizens of Heaven above.
Let His love flow out to others,
Let them fear a Father's care.
That they too may know His welcome
And His countless blessings share.

Church of God, elect and Holy
Be the people He intends;
Strong in faith and swift to answer
Each command your master sends;
Royal priests, fulfil your calling
Through your sacrifice and prayer;

Give your lives in joyful service—
Sing His praise, His love declare.
　　　　　　　— © James E. Seddon

Prayer

O God, my Heavenly Father, You know all about my past, which I confess to you and of which I thoroughly repent. I do not want to live selfishly, I want to redeem the time knowing that the task is urgent, and I pray for Your help and ability to bring to the Saviour my close relatives and anyone else that I can. I know destruction is so near to so many but, Lord, please use me as a soul-winner not only to dwell in the place of safety, but to bring many others to know Jesus as I do. I pray in Jesus' name. Amen.

My personal prayer:

....

....

....

....

....

....

Week 7

Matthew 5:43-44

You have heard that it was said, 'You shall love your neighbour and hate your enemy.' But I say to you, love your enemies, bless those who curse you, do good to those who hate you, and pray for those who spitefully use you and persecute you ...

1 Timothy 2:1-4

Therefore I exhort first of all that supplications, prayers, intercessions, and giving of thanks be made for all men, for kings and all who are in authority, that we may lead a quiet and peaceable life in all godliness and reverence. For this is good and acceptable in the sight of God our Saviour, who desires all men to be saved and come to the knowledge of the truth.

Meditation

In these passages we are directly told to pray specifically for certain people: those who spitefully use or persecute us; for kings and all in authority; indeed for all men and women. I am not sure that we are good at keeping these commands! In 1 Timothy, praying for these people is linked with God's desire to see all of them saved. Reducing individuals to mere numbers leaves us feeling insignificant. Let us learn to pray for our royal family, for political and spiritual leaders, for those who control the media, education, the economy and those who influence the minds of millions. Skevington Wood remarked once that 'It is the temptation of this pragmatic age to presume that technique is the secret of evangelism'. It is not. Only God can make our proclamation fruitful. The resemblance between some evangelistic work and business and sales campaigns undermines what we evangelicals are saying. Let us ask God to allow us to live in an atmosphere which enhances the gospel, but above all, we can pray that these people who need the Lord, just as we do, will be saved. Do they seem too far away from Him for that? Remember, Jesus Christ came into the world to save sinners. They, and we, qualify!

Out in the darkness,
Shadowed by sin,
Souls are in bondage,
Souls we would win.
How can we win them?
How show the way?
Love never fails,
Love is the way.

Think how the Master
Came from above
Suffered on Calvary
Breathing out love;

Think how He loves us,
Even when we stray.
We must love others,
Love is His way.

See, they are waiting,
Looking at you,
Furtively watching
All that you do:
Seeming so careless,
Hardened and lost.
Love never fails
Count not the cost.

Love never fails
Love is pure gold;
Love is what Jesus
Came to unfold,
Make us more loving,
Master, we pray;
Help us remember
Love is God's way.

— FLORA KIRKLAND

Prayer

O Lord God, King of kings and Lord of lords, I pray today for those who have authority on earth. I pray for our royal family: the Queen, Princes and Princesses. In Your goodness please reveal Yourself to them, that they might bow their knees to Your absolute reign over all. Bless them and do them good. I pray for local and national political leaders, asking that they would be given wisdom to lead our nation in godly ways where righteousness and justice rule. Save them I ask. And for those who are my enemies, and enemies of the gospel, please be merciful to them. Lovingly rebuke them, so that they too might repent and believe. Thank you that I live in the times You have allotted for me and I ask to be faithful and loving in proclaiming Jesus to all. Amen.

My personal prayer:

....

....

....

....

....

....

Week 8

Acts 1:1-8

The former account I made, O Theophilus, of all that Jesus began both to do and teach, until the day in which He was taken up, after He through the Holy Spirit had given commandments to the apostles whom He had chosen, to whom He also presented Himself alive after His suffering by many infallible proofs, being seen by them during forty days and speaking of the things pertaining to the kingdom of God. And being assembled together with them, He commanded them not to depart from Jerusalem, but to wait for the Promise of the Father, 'which,' He said, 'you have heard from Me; for John truly baptised with water, but you shall be baptised with the Holy Spirit not many days from now.' Therefore, when they had come together, they asked Him, saying, 'Lord, will You at this time restore the kingdom to Israel?' And He said to them, 'It is not for you to know times or seasons which the Father has put in His own authority. But you shall receive power when the Holy Spirit has come upon you; and you shall be witnesses to Me in Jerusalem, and in all Judea and Samaria, and to the end of the earth.'

Meditation

Like a church bell tolling out a message, this powerful passage strikingly reminds us that God has a strategy for world evangelisation. With the power of the Holy Spirit we are to be witnesses to Jesus first in the immediate area, then to move out of our comfort zone to those increasingly distant from our home, until eventually the gospel has been taken to the very ends of the earth. As witnesses, we do not speak of ourselves but Jesus; not of what we have gained, but of Jesus; not of our particular church or denomination but Jesus. Or, as I once heard the black preacher E. V. Hill say, 'Preach Jesus; He is preachable!' And in proclaiming Christ, we must not just keep Him in the security of the four walls of our churches but witness to Him wherever there is opportunity to do so.

From Greenland's icy mountains,
From India's coral strand,
Where Afric's sunny fountains
Roll down the golden sand,
From many an ancient river,
From many a palmy plain,
They call us to deliver
Their land from error's chain.

What though the spicy breezes
Blow soft o'er Ceylon's isle,
Though every prospect pleases
And only man is vile:
In vain with lavish kindness
The gifts of God are strown;

The heathen in his blindness
Bows down to wood and stone.

Can we, whose souls are lighted
With wisdom from on high,
Can we to men benighted
The lamp of life deny?
Salvation! O Salvation!
The joyful sound proclaim,
Till each remotest nation
Has learned Messiah's name.

Waft, waft, ye winds, his story,
And you, ye waters, roll,
Till, like a sea of glory,
It spreads from pole to pole;
Till o'er our ransomed nature
The Lamb for sinners slain,
Redeemer, King, Creator,
In bliss returns to reign.

— BISHOP HEBER

Prayer

O God, You are truly great. There is no other but
You; three Persons in one, and One in three. You
are Father, Son and Holy Spirit. Heavenly Father,
You sent the Son to be the Saviour of the world.
Lord Jesus, You have lived, died and risen from
the dead that You might be Lord, and more. You
have assured me of the Holy Spirit's presence
and power to go into the far ends of the earth
to be witness of Jesus. What more equipping do
I need? May I be obedient to Your call, and in
straightforward submission live to speak of Jesus.
Amen.

My personal prayer:

....

....

....

....

....

....

Week 9

Acts 1:1-8

The former account I made, O Theophilus, of all that Jesus began both to do and teach, until the day in which He was taken up, after He through the Holy Spirit had given commandments to the apostles whom He had chosen, to whom He also presented Himself alive after His suffering by many infallible proofs, being seen by them during forty days and speaking of the things pertaining to the kingdom of God. And being assembled together with them, He commanded them not to depart from Jerusalem, but to wait for the Promise of the Father, 'which,' He said, 'you have heard from Me; 'for John truly baptized with water, but you shall be baptized with the Holy Spirit not many days from now.' Therefore, when they had come together, they asked Him, saying, 'Lord, will You at this time restore the kingdom to Israel?' And He said to them, 'It is not for you to know times or seasons which the Father has put in His own authority. 'But you shall receive power when the Holy Spirit has come upon you; and you shall be witnesses to Me in Jerusalem, and in all Judea and Samaria, and to the end of the earth.'

Meditation

Jesus was speaking to His disciples just before His ascension where He was taken up, as a cloud took Him out of their sight. The Holy Spirit would empower these early Christians to take the gospel out in ever-extending concentric circles, from their immediate area to the end of the earth. Acts gives us six progress reports as to how this happened.[1] Within a generation the people who were accused of turning the world upside down had penetrated the high echelons of Roman society. The same commission is surely ours today, and the Holy Spirit still gives strength for the task of taking the gospel to ever extending groups of people. Campbell Morgan reflected that to call a person evangelical, who is not evangelistic, is an utter contradiction. I heard a testimony recently from an ex-pop star/alcoholic. What I found so striking and challenging is that he repeatedly said that God always had an answer to all his problems, but nobody had told him what it was. The early church could not be accused of such silence.

Facing a task unfinished
That drives us to our knees,
A need that, undiminished,
Rebukes our slothful ease,
We, who rejoice to know Thee,
Renew before Thy throne
The solemn pledge we owe
To go and make Thee known.

1. Acts 6:7; 9:31; 12:24; 16:5; 19:20; 28:31.

Where other lords beside Thee
Hold their unhindered sway,
Where forces that defied Thee
Defy Thee still today;
With none to heed their crying
For life, and love, and light,
Unnumbered souls are dying
And pass into the night.

We bear the torch that flaming
Fell from the hands of those
Who gave their lives proclaiming
That Jesus died and rose,
Ours is the same commission,
The same glad message ours,
Fired by the same ambition,
To Thee we yield our powers.

O Father who sustained them,
O Spirit who inspired,
Saviour, whose love constrained them
To toil with zeal untired,
From cowardice defend us,
From lethargy awake!
Forth on Thine errands send us
To labour for Thy sake.

— FRANK HOUGHTON

Prayer

O God, It is so challenging to read about the rapid spread of the gospel in those early decades after Jesus' ascension to heaven. I am humbled by the dogged determination to proclaim Christ despite difficulties, divisions and persecutions. Forgive my cowardice and lethargy; teach me again that

You still save people and multiply disciples and churches, and please use me to reach out to someone with the hope and power of the gospel. Prosper the work of evangelism in my locality and county, in my country and continent and to the utmost part of the world. I pray in Jesus' name. Amen.

My personal prayer:

....

....

....

....

....

....

Week 10

Mark 16:15, 16 & 20

A nd He said to them [eleven of the disciples], 'Go into all the world and preach the gospel to every creature. He who believes and is baptised will be saved, but he who does not believe will be condemned' ... And they went out and preached everywhere ...

Meditation

Evangelism is proclaiming the gospel to non-Christians who are listening. It must be the gospel, or good news, that focuses attention on the Lord Jesus Christ, and what He has done for us by His death and resurrection. And the evangelistic preaching whether one to one, or one to a crowd, must be to people who are unconverted. The challenge is to gain the ear of these people so that they listen, first to our voice, and then to the voice of God through His Word. We are under marching orders from the Lord Himself to get out this message to *every* individual. The evangelist, D. L. Moody, as well as the founder of the Navigators, plus many others, never let a day go by without speaking to someone about Jesus. I find deeply challenging the words of New Tribes Mission: 'When people have the choice to choose God, that's their business. When people don't have a choice, it's our business.'

Every person in every nation
In each succeeding generation
Has the right to hear the news
That Christ can save.
Crucified on Calvary's mountain
He opened wide the cleansing fountain
Conquered sin and death and hell,
He rose up from the grave.
Father I am willing to dedicate to Thee
Life and talent, time and money;
Here am I send me.
— Wycliffe Bible Translators

Prayer

Sovereign Lord of heaven and earth, You give to all people life, breath and all things. You have made from one blood every nation of men to dwell on the face of the earth, and You desire that every creature would hear the gospel, for You will that none should perish, but that all should come to repentance and faith in Jesus Christ. Forgive me for my reticence to speak when I ought and help me to be part of that ongoing tide of making known the most wonderful message of Jesus and His love to all. I pray in Jesus' name. Amen.

My personal prayer:

....

....

....

....

....

....

Week 11

Acts 13:1-4

*N*ow *in the church that was at Antioch there were certain prophets and teachers: Barnabas, Simeon who was called Niger, Lucius of Cyrene, Manaen who had been brought up with Herod the tetrarch, and Saul. As they ministered to the Lord and fasted, the Holy Spirit said, 'Now separate to Me Barnabas and Saul for the work to which I have called them.' Then, having fasted and prayed, and laid hands on them, they sent them away. So, being sent out by the Holy Spirit, they went down to Seleucia, and from there they sailed to Cyprus.*

Meditation

Emil Brunner said, 'One who receives the Word, and by it salvation, receives along with it the duty of passing on this Word … Where there is no mission, there is no Church, and where there is neither Church nor mission, there is no faith'. The need for gospel workers in the harvest fields of the world is very great indeed. There are still nations where the name of Jesus is hardly known. That means that there are millions held in the darkness of spiritual ignorance. Others follow religions which are on the false trail of working towards their god(s) and the deluded hope of trying to earn their salvation, failing to understand that heaven is not a reward but a gift. Each generation of Christians has the responsibility to reach its generation with the gospel. If we do not, no one else ever will, for a new generation will have come. The early church, praying and waiting on God to direct them, challenges us to follow their example, and give our very best people to serve the Lord across the world. What greater privilege is there than devoting one's life to making known the Lord of all glory?

We rest on Thee, our Shield and our Defender!
We go not forth alone against the foe;
Strong in Thy strength, safe in Thy keeping tender,
'We rest on Thee and in Thy Name we go.'

Yes, in Thy Name, O Captain of salvation!
In Thy dear Name, all other names above;
Jesus our Righteousness, our sure Foundation,
Our Prince of glory and our King of love.

We go in faith, our own great weakness feeling,
And needing more each day Thy grace to know;
Yet from our hearts a song of triumph pealing,
'We rest on Thee and in Thy Name we go.'

We rest on Thee, our Shield and our Defender!
Thine is the battle, Thine shall be the praise.
When passing through the gates of pearly splendour,
Victors we rest with Thee, through endless days.
— EDITH ADELINE GILLING CHERRY

These words have been etched into Christian consciousness as those sung in January 1956, as five pioneer missionaries working with Wycliffe Bible Translators, made their approach to reach the untouched Auca Indians. The five men were martyred.

Prayer

Heavenly Father, I know that 'the battle' is the Lord's, and remembering the Auca missionaries, I know that what appears tragedy is never lost. Thank you that You never waste any pain, any tears, any toil, nor any time. I praise You that saving men and women is Your work, not mine, and so I look to You to give the increase, so that there will be reaping as well as sowing. I pray in the precious name of Jesus. Amen.

My personal prayer:

....

....

....

....

....

....

Week 12

Ezekiel 3:4-7

*T*hen He said to me: 'Son of man, go to the house of Israel and speak with My words to them. For you are not sent to a people of unfamiliar speech and of hard language, but to the house of Israel, not to many people of unfamiliar speech and of hard language, whose words you cannot understand. Surely, had I sent you to them, they would have listened to you. But the house of Israel will not listen to you, because they will not listen to Me; for all the house of Israel are impudent and hard-hearted.*

Ezekiel 37:1-10

*T*he hand of the LORD came upon me and brought me out in the Spirit of the LORD, and set me down in the midst of the valley; and it was full of bones. Then He caused me to pass by them all around, and behold, there were very many in the open valley; and indeed they were very dry. And He said to me, 'Son of man, can these bones live?' So I answered, 'O LORD GOD, You know.' Again He said to me, 'Prophesy to these bones, and say to them, "O dry bones, hear the word of the LORD! Thus says the*

LORD GOD to these bones: 'Surely I will cause breath to enter into you, and you shall live. I will put sinews on you and bring flesh upon you, cover you with skin and put breath in you; and you shall live. Then you shall know that I am the LORD.'" So I prophesied as I was commanded; and as I prophesied, there was a noise, and suddenly a rattling; and the bones came together, bone to bone. Indeed, as I looked, the sinews and the flesh came upon them, and the skin covered them over; but there was no breath in them. Also He said to me, 'Prophesy to the breath, prophesy, son of man, and say to the breath, "Thus says the LORD GOD: 'Come from the four winds, O breath, and breathe on these slain, that they may live.'" So I prophesied as He commanded me, and breath came into them, and they lived, and stood upon their feet, an exceedingly great army.

Meditation

Imagine you were Ezekiel and were placed in a valley surrounded by dead, dry, decaying bones. Then Almighty God asks you the question, 'Can these dry bones live?' It would seem presumptuous to say they could and unbelieving to respond negatively. Diplomatically, Ezekiel replies by saying that God knows the answer! Notice though, how life comes from death. Ezekiel first preaches the Word, and there is movement, rattling and bones come together and form a mighty army, first of skeletons then of corpses. Then God tells him to speak to the wind, the breath, the Spirit, and suddenly life comes into the corpses and there is a mighty living army all around him.

Note the abiding principle here:

The Word of God + The Spirit of God = New Life or New Birth.

What is needed to bring spiritual life where there is currently death, is the Word of God, taken by the Holy Spirit, who comes when we pray. Evangelist D. L. Moody reminded us: 'There is no better evangelist in the world than the Holy Spirit.'

For my sake, and the gospel's, go
and tell redemption's story';
His heralds answer, 'Be it so,
and thine, Lord, all the glory!'
They preach his birth, his life, his cross,
the love of his atonement,
for whom they count the world but loss,
his Easter, his enthronement.

Hark, hark, the trump of jubilee
proclaims to every nation,
from pole to pole, by land and sea,
glad tidings of salvation;
as nearer draws the day of doom,
while still the battle rages,
the heavenly Dayspring through the gloom
breaks on the night of ages.

Still on and on the anthems spread
of alleluia voices,
in concert with the holy dead
the warrior church rejoices;
their snow white robes are washed in blood,
their golden harps are ringing;

earth and the paradise of God
one triumph song are singing.

— Edward Henry Bickersteth

Prayer

O God, Giver of life, and Spirit of life, I pray for Your help to faithfully proclaim, in every way possible, the Word of God. By Your Holy Spirit please take hold of the Word, and use it to bring new life where once there was death. Please do what only You can do, and continue the work giving newness of life to those who are perishing. I pray in the name of Jesus. Amen.

My personal prayer:

....

....

....

....

....

....

Week 13
John 4:34-38

*J*esus said to them, 'My food is to do the will of Him who sent Me, and to finish His work. Do you not say, "There are still four months and then comes the harvest"? Behold, I say to you, lift up your eyes and look at the fields, for they are already white for harvest! And he who reaps receives wages, and gathers fruit for eternal life, that both he who sows and he who reaps may rejoice together. For in this the saying is true: "One sows and another reaps." I sent you to reap that for which you have not laboured; others have laboured, and you have entered into their labours.'

Luke 10:2

*T*hen He said to them, 'The harvest truly is great, but the labourers are few; therefore pray the Lord of the harvest to send out labourers into His harvest.'

Meditation

To look on the fields and see them white all ready to harvest is deeply moving, but if labourers are few, the scene becomes distressing. The harvest is ready to reap or to rot. Millions are empty, lost and heading for an eternity without Christ which is worse than we can ever imagine. Jesus here specifically tells us for what to pray. He understands the serious need for evangelists. Jesus does not here say that we should pray for more prophets, pastors or priests. The great Bible teacher, C. H. Spurgeon, explained why, 'I would sooner pluck one single brand from the burning than explain all mysteries.' So let us think of particular mission fields at home and abroad; amongst different people groups, and pray that God will send out labourers into those harvest fields. If some areas appear closed, then let us pray that God will open up those harvest fields. When Jesus told us to pray in this way, He was saying that we can speak with God, who influences history, changes nations, and acts in answer to prayer.

Oh, where are the reapers that garner in
The sheaves of the good from the fields of sin?
With sickles of truth must the work be done,
And no one may rest till the 'harvest home.'

Where are the reapers? Oh who will come
And share in the glory of the 'harvest home'?
Oh, who will help us to garner in
The sheaves of good from the fields of sin?

Go out in the byways and search them all:
The wheat may be there, though the weeds are tall;
Then search in the highway, and pass none by,
But gather from all for the home on high.

The fields are all ripening and, far and wide
The world now is waiting the harvest tide;

But reapers are few, and the work is great,
And much will be lost should the harvest wait.

So come with your sickles, you sons of men,
And gather together the golden grain:
Toil on till the Lord of the harvest come,
Then share in the joy of the 'harvest home'.

— E. E. REXFORD

Prayer

Lord of the harvest, You only know the vastness and the greatness of the need. We long to know more of the height and depth, the length and breadth of Your love. But there are millions who know nothing of the gospel at all. I pray that in grace and with urgency You would raise up and send out labourers into the harvest fields around me, in my country, in lands where there is already a harvest, and places where Your name is hardly known. I pray in the name of Jesus. Amen.

My personal prayer:

....

....

....

....

....

....

Week 14

Mark 4:21-25

A *lso He said to them, 'Is a lamp brought to be put under a basket or under a bed? Is it not to be set on a lamp stand? For there is nothing hidden which will not be revealed, nor has anything been kept secret but that it should come to light. If anyone has ears to hear, let him hear.'*

Then He said to them, 'Take heed what you hear. With the same measure you use, it will be measured to you; and to you who hear, more will be given. For whoever has, to him more will be given; but whoever does not have, even what he has will be taken away from him.'

Meditation

In witnessing, there has to be willingness. When there is willingness, God is able to increase winning ways. The young, enthusiastic Christian can at times be an embarrassment to the older, mature believer, but God gives more to those who show an attitude of using the talents He has already bestowed on His child. Winsomeness and dependence upon God will characterize the Christian who has been reading the Word and seeking to reflect Jesus in all that they say or do. Some Christians are wary about sharing their faith, fearing that they could be asked a question they don't know how to answer, and so will let down the Lord Himself. Actually, there are very few questions that people ask anyway and we soon find that we become increasingly equipped to answer them, whilst still pointing people to Christ. So in witnessing, like in fishing, we become more skilled with much practice. Billy Graham put it this way: 'We are the Bibles the world is reading; we are the creed the world is needing; we are the sermons the world is heeding.'

Speak just a word for Jesus,
Tell how He died for you,
Often repeat the story,
Wonderful, glad and true!

> *Speak just a word,*
> *Ever to Him be true;*
> *Speak just a word,*
> *Tell what He's doing for you!*

Speak just a word for Jesus,
Tell how He helps you live,
Tell of the strength and comfort
Which He will freely give!

Speak just a word for Jesus,
Do not for others wait;
Gladly proclaim the message
Ere it shall be too late.

Speak just a word for Jesus —
Why should you doubt or fear?

Surely His love will bless it;
Someone will gladly hear.

Speak just a word for Jesus,
Tell of His love for men!
Someone distressed may listen,
Willing to trust Him then.

— KATHERINE O. BARKER

Prayer

Heavenly Father, I recognise that I have received so much from Your wide open, generous hand and, therefore, my responsibility is great. I want to live a holy life. I want all that I have received to be given back to You. I long for my gifts and abilities, my energy and enthusiasm, my passion and my life, my words and my works to be vivid proclamations of Your love for those around me. Fill me with Your Spirit, give me Your heart, and may I speak as Jesus would have done to those whom I meet. Amen.

My personal prayer:

....

....

....

....

....

....

Week 15

Luke 14:16-24

T *hen He said to him, 'A certain man gave a great supper and invited many, and sent his servant at supper time to say to those who were invited, "Come, for all things are now ready." But they all with one accord began to make excuses. The first said to him, "I have bought a piece of ground, and I must go and see it. I ask you to have me excused." And another said, "I have bought five yoke of oxen, and I am going to test them. I ask you to have me excused." Still another said, "I have married a wife, and therefore I cannot come." So that servant came and reported these things to his master. Then the master of the house, being angry, said to his servant, "Go out quickly into the streets and lanes of the city, and bring in here the poor and the maimed and the lame and the blind." And the servant said, "Master, it is done as you commanded, and still there is room." Then the master said to the servant, "Go out into the highways and hedges, and compel them to come in, that my house may be filled. For I say to you that none of those men who were invited shall taste my supper.'*

Meditation

In all our contact with people, there are three distinct types of individuals. They are seen in this parable. First, there are those you would expect to come to the gospel banquet. They know the gospel, they have already received the invitation, and it would be expected that they would respond. Sadly, instead many simply make excuses. Secondly, there are those who need to be persuaded to come. They can hardly believe that the Lord would want them because they are poor, maimed, lame or blind. They need telling that Jesus came into the world to save sinners and they qualify. Thirdly, there are those who have to be compelled to come to the gospel banquet. They need getting by the scruff of their neck and almost dragging to the feast. But when they are there, how delighted they will be. Treating each person as an individual, with their particular needs, is part of wise soul winning. Some need gentle persuasion, but others need a godly shove towards the Lord. I am reminded of William Booth's motto: 'Go for souls, and go for the worst.'

Out in the highways and byways of life,
Many are weary and sad;
Carry the sunshine where darkness is rife,
Making the sorrowing glad.

Make me a blessing, make me a blessing,
Out of my life may Jesus shine;
Make me a blessing, O Saviour, I pray,
Make me a blessing to someone today.

Tell the sweet story of Christ and His love,
Tell of His power to forgive;
Others will trust Him if only you prove
True, every moment you live.

Give as 'twas given to you in your need,
Love as the Master loved you;
Be to the helpless a helper indeed,
Unto your mission be true.
— IRA B. WILSON

Prayer

Lord, it breaks my heart that those who should have trusted You, make excuses as to why they won't. But then there are others who feel excluded from the feast which is the gospel. They may never pray for themselves but I pray for them. Teach me to be sensitive to each person whom I meet. Help me to be a soul-winner, bringing all types of people to the Lord Jesus. I pray for His glory alone. Amen.

My personal prayer:

....

....

....

....

....

....

The Great Commission and the Need of the People

Week 16

Romans 10:1, 14-15

*B*rethren, my heart's desire and prayer to God for Israel *is* that they may be saved. ... How then shall they call on Him in whom they have not believed? And how shall they believe in Him of whom they have not heard? And how shall they hear without a preacher? And how shall they preach unless they are sent? As it is written: 'How beautiful are the feet of those who preach the gospel of peace, who bring glad tidings of good things!'

Meditation

The Apostle Paul here expresses his deep burden for his own people. It is similar to that of Moses, praying that God would blot out his name; or Jeremiah weeping for the lostness of his people, or that of Jesus weeping over Jerusalem. Paul has a deep down heaviness of heart. He doesn't throw up his hands in horror or go around churches grumbling about the spiritual state of his own people. He prays. He turns his burden over to the Lord. The only answer he knows is the only one there is; that is for people to hear the gospel. People need to be set aside to preach the good news. There is nothing more significant, nothing more enduring, nothing more beautiful than telling others how they can be saved. William Bramwell asked the question, 'How is it the soul being of such value, and God so great, eternity so near and yet we are so little moved?'

Lord, speak to me, that I may speak
In living echoes of Thy tone;
As Thou hast sought, so let me seek
Thy erring children lost and lone.

Oh, lead me, Lord, that I may lead
The wand'ring and the erring feet;
Oh, feed me, Lord, that I may feed
Thy hungry ones with manna sweet.

Oh, teach me, Lord, that I may teach
The precious things Thou dost impart;
And wing my words, that they may reach
The hidden depths of many a heart.

Oh, give Thine own sweet rest to me,
That I may speak with soothing power
A word in season, as from Thee,
To weary ones in needful hour.

Oh, fill me with Thy fullness, Lord,
Until my very heart o'erflow
In kindling thought and glowing word,
Thy love to tell, Thy praise to show.

Oh, use me, Lord, use even me,
Just as Thou wilt, and when, and where,
Until Thy blessed face I see,
Thy rest, Thy joy, Thy glory share.

— Frances R. Havergal

Prayer

O God, You are the Creator of all and yet we know that so many are without Christ and therefore without hope. We pray for those who do not pray for themselves. We pray for their salvation. Our heart cry is still for Israel to be saved. We pray too, for our nation to be saved and we pray that You would call out a people whose priority it is to preach the gospel to the unconverted. We thank you for those throughout history who have been faithful and used in evangelistic work. But we pray that a new generation of gospel workers would be separated to give their lives to this great work. In Jesus' name. Amen.

My personal prayer:

....

....

....

....

....

....

Week 17

Matthew 28:18-20

*A*nd Jesus came and spoke to them, saying, 'All authority has been given to Me in heaven and on earth. Go therefore and make disciples of all the nations, baptising them in the name of the Father and of the Son and of the Holy Spirit, teaching them to observe all things that I have commanded you; and lo, I am with you always, even to the end of the age.'

2 Timothy 2:1-2

*Y*ou therefore, my son, be strong in the grace that is in Christ Jesus. And the things that you have heard from me among many witnesses, commit these to faithful men who will be able to teach others also.

Meditation

In the Great Commission, the title we give to these words of Jesus, He links evangelism with disciple-making. Winning people to Jesus is much easier than seeing these converts become soldiers of Christ and soul-winners themselves. Paul, writing to Timothy, has four generations of Christians: Paul to

Timothy; Timothy to faithful men; faithful men to others. The Lord Jesus spent three years ministering to thousands, but also teaching and modelling godly living to a group of twelve men. The Apostle Paul preached, then taught the new converts, and when he moved on, he prayed for them, sent friends to further instruct and lead them, and wrote letters to them. He saw young Christians as his joy and crown of rejoicing. It is said of John Wesley that although he had no physical children, he had 100,000 spiritual sons and daughters. It is he who said to his workers, 'You have nothing to do, but to save souls; therefore spend and be spent in this work.' Is there any joy to be compared with that of soul-winning and disciple-making?

Go forth and tell! O Church of God, awake!
God's saving news to all the nations take;
Proclaim Christ Jesus, Saviour, Lord and King,
That all the world His worthy praise may sing.

Go forth and tell! God's love embraces all;
He will in grace respond to all who call:
How shall they call if they have never heard
The gracious invitation of His Word?

Go forth and tell where still the darkness lies;
In wealth or want, the sinner surely dies:
Give us, O Lord, concern of heart and mind,
A love like Yours which cares for all mankind.

Go forth and tell! The doors are open wide;
Share God's good gift—let no one be denied;
Live out your life as Christ your Lord shall choose,
Your ransomed powers for His sole glory use.

> Go forth and tell! O Church of God, arise!
> Go in the strength which Christ your Lord
> supplies;
> Go till all nations His great name adore
> And serve Him, Lord and King for evermore.
> — JAMES EDWARD SEDDON

Prayer

Lord God, Thank you that in Your goodness You are willing to use even me in the great working of pointing others to Jesus Christ. Would You help me to both sensitively and boldly share my faith with others. Give me faith to believe that I can be used to win people to Jesus. I need Your wisdom that I may be a good spiritual midwife to men and women in whose lives You are at work. Then, please, give me the diligence and care to help these newly born-again spiritual babes to grow to Christian maturity and become established in a helpful church. Amen.

My personal prayer:

....

....

....

....

....

....

Week 18

Luke 24:13-36

*N*ow that same day two of them were going to a village
called Emmaus, about seven miles from Jerusalem.
*They were talking with each other about everything that
had happened. As they talked and discussed these things
with each other, Jesus himself came up and walked along
with them; but they were kept from recognizing him.*

*He asked them, 'What are you discussing together as
you walk along?'*

*They stood still, their faces downcast. One of them,
named Cleopas, asked him, 'Are you only a visitor to
Jerusalem and do not know the things that have happened
there in these days?'*

'What things?' he asked.

*'About Jesus of Nazareth,' they replied. 'He was a
prophet, powerful in word and deed before God and all
the people. The chief priests and our rulers handed him
over to be sentenced to death, and they crucified him;
but we had hoped that he was the one who was going
to redeem Israel. And what is more, it is the third day
since all this took place. In addition, some of our women
amazed us. They went to the tomb early this morning*

but didn't find his body. They came and told us that they had seen a vision of angels, who said he was alive. Then some of our companions went to the tomb and found it just as the women had said, but him they did not see.'

He said to them, 'How foolish you are, and how slow of heart to believe all that the prophets have spoken! Did not the Christ have to suffer these things and then enter his glory?' And beginning with Moses and all the Prophets, he explained to them what was said in all the Scriptures concerning himself.

As they approached the village to which they were going, Jesus acted as if he were going farther. But they urged him strongly, 'Stay with us, for it is nearly evening; the day is almost over.' So he went in to stay with them.

When he was at the table with them, he took bread, gave thanks, broke it and began to give it to them. Then their eyes were opened and they recognized him, and he disappeared from their sight. They asked each other, 'Were not our hearts burning within us while he talked with us on the road and opened the Scriptures to us?'

They got up and returned at once to Jerusalem. There they found the Eleven and those with them, assembled together and saying, 'It is true! The Lord has risen and has appeared to Simon.' Then the two told what had happened on the way, and how Jesus was recognized by them when he broke the bread.

While they were still talking about this, Jesus himself stood among them and said to them, 'Peace be with you.'

Meditation

Ada Habersheim penned the now-forgotten hymn 'Jesus Himself drew near ...' based on the resurrection appearance of Jesus to the two on the road to Emmaus. But according to Luke 24, Jesus drew near to them twice. First, as they were walking, then later when they had hastily returned to Jerusalem and excitedly told the Eleven disciples what had happened. We read, 'Now as they said these things, Jesus Himself stood in the midst of them.' Isn't this encouraging, that as the two testified, Jesus was there to be with them? He always is! Whether we are testifying, witnessing, preaching, the Lord promises to be with us to encourage, strengthen and use us.

We know little about these two disciples, yet Jesus drew alongside *them*. The Great Commission and the huge need of millions in different cultures and countries is such that it will need every Christian and every gift that the Lord has given to be used in fulfilling the command of Jesus. This is not the time for twiddling thumbs. All leave is cancelled, everyone is needed to make the gospel known to all.

❧

He was not willing that any should perish,
Jesus enthroned in the glory above,
Saw our poor fallen world, pitied our sorrows,
Poured out His life for us, wonderful love!
Perishing, perishing! Thronging our pathway,
Hearts break with burdens too heavy to bear:
Jesus would save, but there's no one to tell them,
No one to lift them from sin and despair.

He was not willing that any should perish:
Clothed in our flesh with its sorrow and pain,
Came He to seek the lost, comfort the mourner,
Heal the heart broken by sorrow and shame,

Perishing, perishing! Harvest is passing,
Reapers are few and the night draweth near:
Jesus is calling you, haste to the reaping,
You shall have souls, precious souls for your hire.

Plenty for pleasure, but little for Jesus;
Time for the world with its troubles and toys,
No time for Jesus' work, feeding the hungry,
Lifting the lost souls to eternity's joys.
Perishing, perishing! Hark how they call us;
Bring us your Saviour, oh tell us of Him!
We are so weary, so heavily laden,
And with long weeping our eyes have grown dim.

He was not willing that any should perish;
Am I His follower, and can I live
Longer at ease with a soul going downward,
Lost for the lack of the help I might give?
Perishing, perishing! You were not willing;
Master, forgive and inspire us anew;
Banish our worldliness, help us to ever
Live with eternity's values in view.

— Lucy R. Meyer

Prayer

Thank you Heavenly Father for the promise of
the Lord Jesus that He will never leave or forsake
me. You go before me, behind me, beside me; You
are above me, below me, and even abide within
me. Thank you that in a very real way, as I seek
to testify, You are there to help, uphold and use
me. Thank you that I am never alone and never
will be. Stir up all in Your church to be mobilised
in the great work of gospel proclamation, I pray.
Amen.

My personal prayer:

....

....

....

....

....

....

Week 19

1 Corinthians 9:16-22

Yet when I preach the gospel, I cannot boast, for I am compelled to preach. Woe to me if I do not preach the gospel! If I preach voluntarily, I have a reward; if not voluntarily, I am simply discharging the trust committed to me. What then is my reward? Just this: that in preaching the gospel I may offer it free of charge, and so not make use of my rights in preaching it. Though I am free and belong to no man, I make myself a slave to everyone, to win as many as possible. To the Jews I became like a Jew, to win the Jews. To those under the law I became like one under the law (though I myself am not under the law), so as to win those under the law. To those not having the law I became like one not having the law (though I am not free from God's law but am under Christ's law), so as to win those not having the law. To the weak I became weak, to win the weak. I have become all things to all men so that by all possible means I might save some.

Meditation

This is a passage packed with principles:

1. Proclaiming the gospel is nothing of which to boast, rather it is the natural thing for a Christian to do.
2. Christians are stewards of the greatest news on earth.
3. Because we are stewards, we are servants to all, and debtors to all—they need us to share the gospel.
4. Paul, as a pattern believer, set the example of refusing to charge for gospel work.
5. As Jesus the Good Shepherd laid down His life for us, so we are to lay down our rights, our life, for others.
6. Indeed we will go to extreme lengths to be able to get alongside people who would not otherwise hear the gospel.

On this last point, I am reminded of the eighteenth century Moravians who sold themselves into slavery that they might reach slaves with the gospel. And today, of a friend of mine who lives in the forests that she might reach eco-warriors for Jesus.

❧

Take my life, and let it be
Consecrated, Lord, to Thee;
Take my moments and my days,
Let them flow in ceaseless praise.

Take my hands, and let them move
At the impulse of Thy love;
Take my feet, and let them be
Swift and beautiful for Thee.

Take my voice, and let me sing
Always, only for my King;
Take my lips, and let them be
Filled with messages from Thee.

Take my silver and my gold,
Not a mite would I withhold;

Take my intellect, and use
Every power as Thou shalt choose.

Take my will, and make it Thine;
It shall be no longer mine;
Take my heart, it is Thine own;
It shall be Thy royal throne.

Take my love; my Lord, I pour
At Thy feet its treasure-store;
Take myself, and I will be
Ever, only, all for Thee!
— FRANCES RIDLEY HAVERGAL

Prayer

O Lord Jesus, You who were rich for our sakes became poor. You, who are God, clothed Yourself with humanity. You were worshipped and adored in heaven, yet allowed Yourself to be crucified. You, the Life, took on Yourself death and for my sake. Teach me afresh the privilege of yielding myself, my rights, my privileges for the sake of others. Take all that I am, all that I have, and all I ever hope to be, and use me for Your glory and the extension of Your kingdom on earth. Amen.

My personal prayer:

....

....

....

....

....

....

Week 20

Ecclesiastes 11:1-6

*C*ast your bread upon the waters, for you will find it after many days. Give a serving to seven, and also to eight, for you do not know what evil will be on the earth. If the clouds are full of rain, they empty themselves upon the earth; and if a tree falls to the south or the north, in the place where the tree falls, there it shall lie. He who observes the wind will not sow, and he who regards the clouds will not reap. As you do not know what is the way of the wind, or how the bones grow in the womb of her who is with child, so you do not know the works of God who makes everything. In the morning sow your seed, and in the evening do not withhold your hand; for you do not know which will prosper, either this or that, or whether both alike will be good.

Meditation

Robert Louis Stevenson said, 'Don't judge each day by the harvest you reap, but by the seeds you plant.' In this passage we are encouraged to sow expecting to reap and, therefore, it makes sense to sow generously, taking every opportunity to speak to people about the Lord Jesus. The opportunities we have now may not be the same in the future. So let us sow just where we are, despite whatever difficulties we may face. God will do His unseen work of bringing a harvest from the seed sown. So let us sow gospel seed at all times, and wait with anticipation to see which will in due time be harvested.

Go quickly, for the fading hours
With haste are sinking to the west;
Exert with zeal your ransomed powers,
Nor think it yet the time for rest.

Go quickly, for the sons of time
Are journeying to a hopeless grave,
And tell to earth's remotest clime
Of Him who came to seek and save.

Go quickly to the realms of sin;
Invite as many as you find;
And welcome all to enter in—
The poor, the maimed, the lame, the blind.

Go quickly with the living Word
Sent to the nations from above,
Till every heart on earth has heard
The tidings of redeeming love.

— WILLIAM WILEMAN

Prayer

Lord, Creator of all, I thank You for the remarkable power of a seed to reproduce after its own. I bless You too that gospel seed simply sown is precious, powerful, and productive in bringing new, eternal life in the hearts of those who believe. Lord, help me to be a sower of this seed, diligent and faithful, as I seek to carefully scatter Your Word at every opportunity. Then, Lord, please do Your work so that the seed will fall on good ground, be well-watered and grow to be seed-bearing fruit itself. I pray this for Your honour alone. Amen.

My personal prayer:

....

....

....

....

....

....

Week 21

2 Corinthians 5:11, 13-15 & 20

Knowing, therefore, the terror of the Lord, we persuade men ... For if we are beside ourselves, it is for God; or if we are of sound mind, it is for you. For the love of Christ compels us, because we judge thus: that if One died for all, then all died; and He died for all, that those who live should live no longer for themselves, but for Him who died for them and rose again ... Now then, we are ambassadors for Christ, as though God were pleading through us: we implore you on Christ's behalf, be reconciled to God.

Meditation

'The love of Christ compels us': is it *our* love for Christ, or *His* love for us? If it appears ambiguous, perhaps it is because both are true. God's love for us is infinite and eternal. It is supremely expressed in Jesus' death for all. For us though, there is such gratitude that we feel overwhelmed with love towards Jesus. Therefore, it is totally inappropriate to live for ourselves. Rather, we want to be God's ambassadors, recognising that this world is not our home, that our citizenship is elsewhere, but in every action we make, and in each word we speak, we are representing Him, who has made us His at such a great price to Himself. Bill Bright, the founder of Campus Crusade for Christ, said, 'Although I have shared Christ personally with thousands of people through the years, I am a rather reserved person and I do not always find it easy to witness. But I have made this my practice, and urge you to do the same: Assume that whenever you are alone with another person for more than a few moments, you are there by divine appointment to explain to that person the love and forgiveness he can know through faith in Jesus Christ.'

'For my sake, and the gospel's, go
and tell redemption's story';
His heralds answer, 'Be it so,
and thine, Lord, all the glory!'
They preach his birth, his life, his cross,
the love of his atonement,
for whom they count the world but loss,
his Easter, his enthronement.

Hark, hark, the trump of jubilee
proclaims to every nation,
from pole to pole, by land and sea,
glad tidings of salvation;
as nearer draws the day of doom,
while still the battle rages,
the heavenly Dayspring through the gloom
breaks on the night of ages.

Still on and on the anthems spread
of alleluia voices,
in concert with the holy dead

the warrior church rejoices;
their snow white robes are washed in blood,
their golden harps are ringing;
earth and the paradise of God
one triumph song are singing.

He comes, whose advent trumpet drowns
the last of time's evangels,
Emmanuel crowned with many crowns,
the Lord of saints and angels;
O Life, Light, Love, the great I AM,
Triune, who changes never,
the throne of God and of the Lamb
is Yours, and Yours forever.

— EDWARD HENRY BICKERSTETH

Prayer

Lord Jesus Christ, Thank you that I belong to You. Thank you for who You are, and for all You have done for me. I rejoice in Your amazing love. I am not my own; I praise You that You have purchased me at such a great price. I want You to know that I love You, and long for this to be evident in the way I live and speak. I desire to glorify You in my body, throughout my life, and to be a good ambassador of Yours. Amen.

My personal prayer:

....

....

....

....

....

....

Week 22

Isaiah 52:7-10

How beautiful upon the mountains are the feet of him who brings good news, who proclaims peace, who brings glad tidings of good things, who proclaims salvation, who says to Zion, 'Your God reigns!' Your watchmen shall lift up their voices, with their voices they shall sing together; for they shall see eye to eye when the LORD *brings back Zion. Break forth into joy, sing together, you waste places of Jerusalem! For the* LORD *has comforted His people, He has redeemed Jerusalem. The* LORD *has made bare His holy arm in the eyes of all the nations; and all the ends of the earth shall see the salvation of our God.*

Meditation

God has always had a heart for nations and people. His desire throughout all ages is that people should know Him and follow in His ways. This is not just a New Testament idea. Notice the parallel thinking throughout this passage: proclaiming and singing; speaking and seeing; peace, glad tidings and salvation; comfort and redemption; Jerusalem and all the ends of the earth. How all-inclusive is the gospel, but then it does come from the very heart of our infinite God whose mercies and compassions never fail. How very gracious is our God to see even feet as beautiful! The least of us is involved in a significant work as we bring good news to others. Writing about the early days of the post-apostolic church, Philip Schaff said, 'While there were no professional missionaries devoting their whole life to this specific work, every congregation was a missionary society, and every Christian believer a missionary, inflamed by the love of Christ to convert his fellow men … Every Christian told his neighbour, the labourer to his fellow labourer, the slave to his fellow slave, the servant to his master and mistress, the story of his conversion as a mariner tells the story of the rescue from shipwreck.'

❧

'Where He leads me I will follow;'
Oft I've sung it blessed Lord,
Oft I've said, with heart o'er-flowing,
I would follow at Thy word.
Now I stand in holy wonder,
Hushed and awed by power divine,
Stand before an open gateway,
With my hand still clasping Thine.

Sacred trust! O, blessed privilege:
Theme befitting angel voice!
Yet to me trust is given,
O, my soul, rejoice, rejoice!
When the God of all creation
Bids me go His love to tell,

Naught in earth or hell can stay me;
Home, and friends, and all, farewell.

Stretching onward, ever onward,
Lo, a slender path I see,
Leading to a land in darkness;
Lord, is that the path for me?
Tremblingly I ask the question;
Hushed, I catch the low reply;
'In the darkness souls are dying,'
Blessed Master, here am I.

'Go, oh quickly go and tell them
Of my death on Calvary's tree;
Lead them to the cleansing fountain
Flowing still, so full and free.
Tell them of that glorious morning
When I left the empty tomb,
Conq'ring death for them for ever;
Tell them I am coming soon.'
— FLORENCE A. HILBORN

Prayer

Heavenly Father, having beautiful feet seems a very strange description of the person I long to be, and yet a proclaimer of good news of peace and of salvation is exactly what I want to be. Anything worthy within me is all of Your doing, and I thank You for Your gracious dealings with me. My desire and prayer is that people might see Your reign, instead of the world's ruin, that they might hear of Your salvation rather than the nations' sin. Turn again the hearts of the people toward Yourself, I pray, in Jesus' name. Amen.

My personal prayer:

....

....

....

....

....

....

The Soul Winners' Motive and the 'Lostness of the Lost'

Week 23

Ezekiel 33:1-11

*A*gain the word of the LORD came to me, saying, 'Son of man, speak to the children of your people, and say to them: "When I bring the sword upon a land, and the people of the land take a man from their territory and make him their watchman, when he sees the sword coming upon the land, if he blows the trumpet and warns the people, then whoever hears the sound of the trumpet and does not take warning, if the sword comes and takes him away, his blood shall be on his own head. He heard the sound of the trumpet, but did not take warning; his blood shall be upon himself. But he who takes warning will save his life. But if the watchman sees the sword coming and does not blow the trumpet, and the people are not warned, and the sword comes and takes any person from among them, he is taken away in his iniquity; but his blood I will require at the watchman's hand." So you, son of man: I have made you a watchman for the house of Israel; therefore you shall hear a word from My mouth and warn them for Me. When I say to the wicked, "O wicked man, you shall surely die!" and you do not speak to warn the wicked* *from his way, that wicked man shall die in his iniquity; but his blood I will require at your hand. Nevertheless if you warn the wicked to turn from his way, and he does not turn from his way, he shall die in his iniquity; but you have delivered your soul. Therefore you, O son of man, say to the house of Israel: "Thus you say, 'If our transgressions and our sins lie upon us, and we pine away in them, how can we then live?' Say to them: "As I live," says the LORD God, "I have no pleasure in the death of the wicked, but that the wicked turn from his way and live. Turn, turn from your evil ways! For why should you die, O house of Israel?"'*

Meditation

With all the joys of knowing Jesus as our Lord and Saviour, we have the awesome responsibility of making known the gospel. Clearly, for we who are in Christ, there is now no condemnation. We are safe when it comes to our eternal home. Nevertheless, there is the judgement seat of Christ, where all our works as Christians will be tried. None of us wants to have the blood of others on our hands. This is the other side to the love of Jesus constraining us. We are under marching orders from our Commander-in-Chief; we are to be as watchmen, warning fellow-citizens of the urgent need to be made right with God; we will give account of how we have used our time and talents, energy and opportunity for the kingdom of God; we will want to be good stewards of the responsibility God has given to us. If God has no pleasure in the death of the wicked, neither can we.

⚜

Jesus, Your blood and righteousness,
My beauty are, my glorious dress,
Midst flaming worlds, in these arrayed,
With joy shall I lift up my head.

Lord, I believe Your precious blood,
Which at the mercy seat of God
For ever does for sinners plead,
For me, even for my soul was shed.

Lord, I believe, were sinners more
Than sands upon the ocean shore
You have for all a ransom paid,
For all a full atonement made.

Ah! Give to all Your servants Lord,
With power to speak Your gracious Word,
That all who to Your wounds will go,
May find eternal life in You.

Oh, let the dead now hear Your voice,
Now bid Your banished ones rejoice,
Their beauty this, their glorious dress,
Jesus, Your blood and righteousness.

— COUNT ZINZENDORF

Prayer

O Holy God, before whom all people will stand,
I praise You for clothing me in the righteousness
of Jesus. And more than simply making me Your
child, You have commissioned me to serve by
speaking and warning others of their need for
salvation. Please forgive me for those many times
I have kept silent when I should have spoken.

Teach me to have a loving boldness, which warns men and women of their need to repent and believe. Deliver me from the scourge of inconsequential chatter, teaching me to be a watchman speaking Your Word to those around me. I pray in Jesus' name. Amen

My personal prayer:

....

....

....

....

....

....

Week 24

Ezekiel 21:9-11

S on of man, prophesy and say, 'Thus says the Lord!'
Say: 'A sword, a sword is sharpened and also polished!
Sharpened to make a dreadful slaughter, polished to flash
like lightning! Should we then make mirth? It despises
the sceptre of My Son, as it does all wood. And He has
given it to be polished, that it may be handled; this sword
is sharpened, and it is polished to be given into the hand
of the slayer.'

Meditation

I find terror in these words. Jim Packer said, 'There
are few things stressed more strongly in the Bible
than the reality of God's work as Judge.' God's anger
is not an uncontrolled passionate outburst nor an
impetuous mood, but a principle, namely the eternal
hatred of sin, and His eternal love of righteousness.
Today's society has a hazy, blurred idea that God is
too kind to punish the ungodly. This is an opiate to
the consciences of millions of sincere people. They
live under a delusion that all will be well, just as did
the British nation before World War II, despite all that

Winston Churchill was warning about. Read these words from Jonathan Edwards' sermon 'Sinners in the hands of an angry God' preached on Sunday, July 8th, 1741: 'O Sinner! Consider the fearful danger. The unconverted are now walking over the pit of hell on a rotten covering, and there are innumerable places in this covering so weak, that it will not bear their weight, and these places are not seen … The wrath of God is now undoubtedly hanging over a great part of this congregation.' Oh, for a heart to see the lost as God sees them, and love them as He loves them!

> Away in the heathen darkness drear,
> Lost souls are born and die in fear.
> They grope to find the light of life,
> To end their misery and strife.
> Oh you who know the way to God,
> Won't you to them the gospel bring?
> Haste then e'er more shall die in sin,
> And tell of Jesus' death for them.
>
> Today some heathen mother dear,
> Is turning from a sacred stream,
> To which she threw her precious child,
> An offering to please her god.
> O you who know the one true God,
> What offering did you bring today?
> You claim to have the peace of God,
> Yet care not they must seek in vain.
>
> Somewhere a man is passing on,
> His life and breath are almost gone.
> His way is dark we know full well,

But no one goes of Christ to tell.
In misery he cries in vain,
Knows not that Jesus died for him.
And in a Christ-less grave he's laid
Forgotten, lost and doomed for hell.

O Christian friends they're dying now,
A hundred thousand souls today.
How shall we face our blessed Lord,
If any longer we delay?
O you who know the way to God,
Won't you to them the gospel bring?
Haste then e'er more shall die in sin,
And tell of Jesus death for them.

— JOHN C. RATZLAFF

Prayer

Dear Heavenly Father, Please forgive my cold-hearted indifference towards the plight of all those with whom I rub shoulders, who are away from You. O dear God, I grieve for those around me who are lost and heading for judgement. Thank you for the love You have showered upon me, but I pray that, instead of selfishly relishing it, I would selflessly demonstrate Your passion in my attitudes and acts, ways and words, longing and love towards everyone with whom I have contact today. I pray in the name of Jesus, Amen.

My personal prayer:

....

....

....

....

....

....

Week 25

Matthew 9:35-38

*T hen Jesus went about all the cities and villages,
teaching in their synagogues, preaching the gospel of
the kingdom, and healing every sickness and every disease
among the people. But when He saw the multi-tudes, He
was moved with compassion for them, because they were
weary and scattered, like sheep having no shepherd. Then
He said to His disciples, 'The harvest truly is plentiful,
but the labourers are few. Therefore pray the Lord of the
harvest to send out labourers into His harvest'.*

Meditation

Jesus did not just minister, without having compassion, nor did He feel emotion without actually serving. They were both vital ingredients of the life of
our Saviour, and Scripture puts them together. Here,
immediately after activity, Jesus encouraged His
disciples to pray. In Luke's Gospel after the parable
of the Good Samaritan where we are told 'to go and
do', we have the Martha and Mary incident which
teaches us to sit at the feet of Jesus. So in this passage
we see that proclamation, acts of mercy, compassion

and prayer all add up to the work of harvesting which is so dear to the heart of Jesus.

Only one life to offer, Jesus my Lord and King;
Only one tongue to praise Thee, and of Your mercy sing;
Only one heart's devotion, Saviour oh, may it be
Consecrated alone to Your matchless glory,
Yielded fully to Thee.

Only this hour is mine Lord; may it be used for Thee;
May every passing moment count for eternity;
Souls all about are dying, dying in sin and shame;
Help me bring them the message of Calvary's redemption
In Thy glorious name.

Only one life to offer, take it dear Lord, I pray;
Nothing from Thee withholding, Your will I now obey;
You who have freely given, Your all in all for me,
Claim this life for Your Son to be used, my Saviour,
Every moment for Thee.

— Avis B. Christiansen

Prayer

O God, Lord of the harvest, I see all around people who are like sheep without a shepherd. They are scattered and lost, following any and all voices, living in danger and away from Your green pastures and still waters. The harvest is plentiful. It is ready to reap, but much is rotting away. I pray then that by Your Holy Spirit, labourers will be stirred to go to the harvest fields of the world to glean and reap; to tell of Jesus, the Good Shepherd who laid down His life for the sheep. Amen.

My personal prayer:

....

....

....

....

....

....

Week 26

2 Corinthians 4:1-5

Therefore, since we have this ministry, as we have received mercy, we do not lose heart. But we have renounced the hidden things of shame, not walking in craftiness nor handling the word of God deceitfully, but by manifestation of the truth commending ourselves to every man's conscience in the sight of God. But even if our gospel is veiled, it is veiled to those who are perishing, whose minds the god of this age has blinded, who do not believe, lest the light of the gospel of the glory of Christ, who is the image of God, should shine on them. For we do not preach ourselves, but Christ Jesus the Lord, and ourselves your bondservants for Jesus' sake.

Meditation

Whether in an enormous crowd watching a sports game, or in a huge meeting place, or simply standing in a busy pedestrian precinct, we are surrounded by teeming crowds, made up of masses of individuals, each with their own personal history, burdens and ambitions. And everyone who has not trusted Jesus as Lord and Saviour is lost. If we could understand the harrowing nature of that word 'lost', we would not only have a glimpse of the heart of God towards those whom He has created, but who have dared to defy and resist Him, but also have a new love for them. As D. T. Niles famously said, 'Evangelism is one beggar telling another beggar where he found bread.'

So send I you to labour unrewarded,
To serve unpaid, unloved, unsought, unknown,
To bear rebuke, to suffer scorn and scoffing—
So send I you to toil for Me alone.

So send I you to bind the bruised and broken,
Over wandering souls to work, to weep, to wake,
To bear the burden of the world a-weary—
So send I you to suffer for My sake.

So send I you to loneliness and longing,
With heart a-hungering for the loved and known
Forsaking home and kindred, friend and dear one—
So send I you to know My love alone.

So send I you to leave your life's ambition
To die to dear desire, self-will resign,
To labour long and love where men revile you—
So send I you to lose your life in Mine.

So send I you to hearts made hard by hatred,
To eyes made blind because they will not see,
To spend, though it be blood, to spend and spare not—
So send I you to taste of Calvary.

'As the Father has sent Me, so send I you.'
— E. Margaret Clarkson

Prayer

Lord Jesus, I remember that You wept over Jerusalem, and at the grave of Lazarus. I know You prayed throughout whole nights, and agonized in the Garden of Gethsemane before Your betrayal and arrest. I am challenged by Your ministry which was so consistent and loving. O God, make me more like Jesus. I pray that the Holy Spirit would fill me, fire me and empower me to go and tell of Jesus, who though He was rich, for our sakes became poor, and died, the Righteous for the unrighteous, that He might bring us to God. Amen.

My personal prayer:

....

....

....

....

....

....

Week 27

Luke 16:19-31

*T*here was a certain rich man who was clothed in purple and fine linen and fared sumptuously every day. But there was a certain beggar named Lazarus, full of sores, who was laid at his gate, desiring to be fed with the crumbs which fell from the rich man's table. Moreover the dogs came and licked his sores. So it was that the beggar died, and was carried by the angels to Abraham's bosom. The rich man also died and was buried. And being in torments in Hades, he lifted up his eyes and saw Abraham afar off, and Lazarus in his bosom. Then he cried and said, 'Father Abraham, have mercy on me, and send Lazarus that he may dip the tip of his finger in water and cool my tongue; for I am tormented in this flame.' But Abraham said, 'Son, remember that in your lifetime you received your good things, and likewise Lazarus evil things; but now he is comforted and you are tormented. And besides all this, between us and you there is a great gulf fixed, so that those who want to pass from here to you cannot, nor can those from there pass to us.' Then he said, 'I beg you therefore, father, that you would send him to my father's house, for I have five brothers, that he may testify to them, lest they also come to this place of torment.' Abraham said to him, 'They have Moses and the prophets; let them hear them.' And he said, 'No, father Abraham; but if one goes to them from the dead, they will repent.' But he said to him, 'If they do not hear Moses and the prophets, neither will they be persuaded though one rise from the dead.'

Meditation

What was the sin of the rich man in this haunting story of Jesus? Was it not that he neglected his neighbour, and in so doing showed that he did not really love God? God places us strategically in different places and situations, and we are there as missionaries. If we do not share Jesus with our neighbours and colleagues, who else will? We wouldn't want to insensitively ram the gospel down the throats of our neighbours, but we can pray for the moment and opportunity to speak, and then be ready for the answer to that specific prayer. A. W. Tozer once said that he 'waited and watched fifteen long years to get my chance to speak with one man. Never a day passed in all those fifteen years that I did not speak to God about that man. At last my chance came, and it was my privilege to lead him to Christ.' How we need the right mix of boldness and sensitivity, of patience and urgency, of the zeal of a mother to give birth and skill of a midwife to secure safety in that birth!

❦

God has His best things for the few
Who dare to stand the test;
God has His second choice for those
Who will not take His best.

It is not always open ill
That risks the promised rest;
The 'better' often is the foe
That keeps us from His best.

And others make the highest choice,
But when, by trials pressed,
They shrink, they yield, they shun the cross,
And so they lose the best.

I want, in this short life of mine,
As much as can be pressed
Of service true for God and man—
Help me to be my best.

I want among the victor-throng
To have my name confessed,
And hear the Master say at last—
'Well done! You did your best.'

Give me, O Lord, Thy highest choice,
Let others take the rest;
Their good things have no charm for me—
For I enjoy Thy Best!

— A. B. SIMPSON

Prayer

O holy God, the rich man and Lazarus lived such
different lives, died very different deaths and now
experience totally different eternities. Forgive me

when I show my lack of love for You by neglecting my neighbour. Teach me true spiritual wisdom and passion, caring for the poor, the underdog, the lost and the deluded. I pray in Jesus' name. Amen.

My personal prayer:

....

....

....

....

....

....

Week 28

Jeremiah 9:1-2

'*O*h, that my head were waters, and my eyes a fountain of tears, that I might weep day and night for
the slain of the daughter of my people! Oh, that I had in
the wilderness a lodging place for travellers; that I might
leave my people, and go from them! For they are all adul-
terers, an assembly of treacherous men.'*

Jeremiah 20:9

*T*hen I said, 'I will not make mention of Him, nor
speak anymore in His name.' But His word was in
my heart like a burning fire shut up in my bones; I was
weary of holding it back, and I could not.*

Meditation

How easily we find ourselves distracted or discouraged so that the main thing, which is to keep the
main thing the main thing, is neglected. If Jeremiah
could find this, so can we! The burden, the passion,
the zeal become tired and worn. When people are
antagonistic to God this is understandable, so we
need to come to the Lord for fresh strength, burden

and vision. The founder of the Salvation Army, William Booth, said, 'While some weep, as they do now, I'll fight; while little children go hungry I'll fight; while men go to prison, in and out, in and out, as they do now, I'll fight; while there is a drunkard left, while there is a poor, lost girl upon the streets, where there remains one dark soul without the light of God—I'll fight! I'll fight to the very end!' So we are called to die to self, to carry a cross, to forsake the world, to suffer, to holiness, to give our lives to the service of God and the saving of the lost. That means crucifying the whims and fears that keep us from naming Jesus; it means asking God to freshly touch our lips to go with messages from God about God to the people that God loves and desires to make His own.

O Thou who camest from above
The pure celestial fire to impart,
Kindle a flame of sacred love
On the mean altar of my heart!

There let it for Thy glory burn
With inextinguishable blaze;
And trembling to its source return,
In humble prayer and fervent praise.

Jesus confirm my heart's desire
To work, and speak, and think for Thee;
Still let me guard the holy fire,
And still stir up Thy gift in me.

Ready for all Thy perfect will,
My acts of faith and love repeat
Till death Thy endless mercies seal,
And make the sacrifice complete.

— CHARLES WESLEY

Prayer

Lord God, in becoming Your child I have become someone who wants to reflect and radiate Your character. I accept friends of Yours, as friends of mine; Your enemies are my enemies; Your ways are to be my ways; Your life is my life and Lord, Your message is my message. May I never be guilty of spin when it comes to presenting the gospel, and may I be filled with strength from above as I do! I pray in Jesus' name. Amen.

My personal prayer:

....

....

....

....

....

....

The Process of Evangelism

Week 29

Matthew 5:14-16

'*You are the light of the world. A city that is set on a hill cannot be hidden. Nor do they light a lamp and put it under a basket, but on a lamp stand, and it gives light to all who are in the house. Let your light so shine before men, that they may see your good works and glorify your Father in heaven*'.

Meditation

I'm not sure that Francis of Assisi really did say, 'Preach the gospel, and if necessary use words', but if he did, he was not giving us a balanced view of the Bible's teaching. God uses words. In fact Matthew 5, which is the beginning of 'The Sermon on the Mount' begins with, 'And seeing the multitudes, [Jesus] went up on a mountain … Then He opened His mouth and taught them, saying … ' But many a Christian testimony has been spoiled by inconsistencies, sins and a lack of integrity from the person witnessing. A godly life and a loving tongue are powerful tools in the hand of our holy God who speaks to men and women through us.

The Israelites annually went through their homes to remove any leaven, a picture on this occasion of sin. Let us follow their example and allow the Lord to remove all taints of sin, godlessness and unrighteousness from our lives and our dealings with others. Paul wrote to Titus saying, 'Those who have believed in God should be careful to maintain good works.' (3:8)

❧

How I praise You, precious Saviour,
That Your love laid hold of me;
You have saved and cleansed and filled me
That I might Your channel be.

    Channels only, blessed Master,
    But with all Thy wondrous power
    Flowing through us, You can use us
    Every day and every hour.

Witnessing Your power to save me,
Setting free from self and sin;
You who bought me to possess me,
In Your fullness, Lord, come in.

Channels only, blessed Master,
But with all Your wondrous power
Flowing through us, You can use us
Every day and every hour.

— Mary E. Maxwell

Prayer

Thank you, holy God, for the wonderful fact that righteousness is not earned, but given to me through the finished work of Christ. May I never abuse such dying love, but rather increasingly learn to put to death all that causes Your wrath, and to put on all that is glorifying to You. May I always remember that 'the grace of God that brings salvation has appeared to all men, teaching us to say "no" to ungodliness and worldly passions and to live self-controlled, upright and godly lives in this present age.' Therefore 'search me, O God, and know my heart; test me, and know my anxious thoughts; see if there is any offensive way in me, and lead me in the way everlasting.' I pray in the name of the Lord Jesus. Amen.

My personal prayer:

....

....

....

....

....

....

Week 30

Mark 4:1-20

*A*nd again He began to teach by the sea. And a great multitude was gathered to Him, so that He got into a boat and sat in it on the sea; and the whole multitude was on the land facing the sea. Then He taught them many things by parables, and said to them in His teaching:

'Listen! Behold, a sower went out to sow. And it happened, as he sowed, that some seed fell by the wayside; and the birds of the air came and devoured it. Some fell on stony ground, where it did not have much earth; and immediately it sprang up because it had no depth of earth. But when the sun was up it was scorched, and because it had no root it withered away. And some seed fell among thorns; and the thorns grew up and choked it, and it yielded no crop. But other seed fell on good ground and yielded a crop that sprang up, increased and produced: some thirtyfold, some sixty, and some a hundred.'

And He said to them, 'He who has ears to hear, let him hear!'

And He said to them, 'Do you not understand this parable? How then will you understand all the parables? The sower sows the word. And these are the ones by the wayside where the word is sown. When they hear, Satan comes immediately and takes away the word that was sown in their hearts. These likewise are the ones sown on stony ground who, when they hear the word, immediately receive it with gladness; and they have no root in themselves, and so endure only for a time. Afterward, when tribulation or persecution arises for the word's sake, immediately they stumble. Now these are the ones sown among thorns; they are the ones who hear the word, and the cares of this world, the deceitfulness of riches, and the desires for other things entering in choke the word, and it becomes unfruitful. But these are the ones sown on good ground, those who hear the word, accept it, and bear fruit: some thirtyfold, some sixty, and some a hundred.'

Meditation

Sowing is a laborious work. Jesus uses this activity to picture work in the kingdom of God. For God's work to get into the hearts of men and women, the Word of God must be sown. The farmer sows, then has to wait and trust that the very gradual work of the seed germinating, taking root and eventually growing and bearing fruit will be done. He may not understand how this happens, but he believes it will. It is a divinely established order that labour and achievement are linked. Therefore, learning from the parable, we must sow the seed of the Word of God. 'Let the redeemed of the Lord say so!'

In the harvest fields now ripened
There's a work for all to do;
'Hark' the voice of God is calling
To the harvest, calling you.

> *Little is much when God is in it;*
> *Labour not for wealth or fame;*
> *There's a crown and you can win it*
> *If you will go in Jesus' name.*

Does the place you're called to labour
Seem so small and little known?
It is grace if God is in it
For He'll not forsake His own.

When the conflict here is ended
And our work on earth is done;
He will say if you are faithful,
'Welcome Home, my child well done!'

— Graham Murphy

Prayer

O God, thank you for the seed of the Word of God. It has worked wonders in my life. Help me to sow it into the lives of many others. And yes, Lord, I know that there will be disappointments, but I pray that much seed will fall on good ground and bring forth much fruit. Please help me to be a faithful sower of the seed, today, and every day. I pray in the altogether worthy name of Jesus. Amen.

My personal prayer:

....

....

....

....

....

....

Week 31

Ephesians 4:11-16

A nd He Himself gave some to be apostles, some prophets, some evangelists, and some pastors and teachers,
for the equipping of the saints for the work of ministry,
for the edifying of the body of Christ, till we all come to
the unity of the faith and of the knowledge of the Son of
God, to a perfect man, to the measure of the stature of the
fullness of Christ; that we should no longer be children,
tossed to and fro and carried about with every wind of
doctrine, by the trickery of men, in the cunning craftiness
of deceitful plotting, but, speaking the truth in love, may
grow up in all things into Him who is the head—Christ—
from whom the whole body, joined and knit together by
what every joint supplies, according to the effective working by which every part does its share, causes growth of
the body for the edifying of itself in love.*

Meditation

Not everyone has the gift of the evangelist. Every
Christian is called to be a witness, to testify as to
what the Lord has done for them, and to share the
gospel with those whom they meet. Paul writes to
his beloved young, timid friend, Timothy, who is a

pastor, that he should 'do the work of the evange- list'. So even though evangelism may not have been Timothy's prime gifting, Paul says that he must not remain 'feeding the flock' of God, but going out and about to find more lost sheep. In the twenty-seven or so gifts or talents that God has given to the church that are listed in the Bible, the evangelist is one of them, and there is no hint that this gift was only for the early church. The evangelist will be deeply bur- dened for unconverted people to come to Christ; show signs of having the ability to win people to Christ; and seek to help equip the church in its evan- gelistic work. Philip, the evangelist, spoke to large crowds and to individuals. He itinerated, and also remained in Caesarea for twenty years. He worked in cities and rural environments. He was a spiritual man, and had the great joy of seeing his family fol- low in his footsteps. Let us pray that God would make us all faithful witnesses, and that He would raise up evangelists who will have the ability to sow and reap souls for Christ.

A band of faithful reapers we,
Who gather for eternity
The golden sheaves of ripened grain
From every valley, hill and plain:
Our song is one the reapers sing
In honour of their Lord and King—
The Master of the harvest wide,
Who for a world of sinners died.

To the harvest field away,
For the Master calls;
There is work for all today,
'Ere the darkness falls:
Swiftly do the moments fly,
Harvest days are going by,
Going, going, going by.

We are a faithful gleaning band,
And labour at our Lord's command;
Unyielding, loyal, tried and true,
For lo! The reapers are but few;
Behold the waving harvest field,
Abundant with a golden yield;
And hear the Lord of harvest say
To all, 'Go reap for Me today!'

The golden hours like moments fly,
And harvest days are passing by;
Then take your rusty sickle down,
And labour for a fadeless crown,
Why will you idly stand and wait?
Behold, the hour is growing late!
Can you to judgement bring but leaves,
While here are waiting golden sheaves?

— CHARLES H. GABRIEL

Prayer

Lord of the harvest, thank You for gifting Your people to serve You and Your church in so many different ways. Help me to seriously obey the call to be a consistent, faithful witness to the things of Christ that I have seen and heard. Please raise up more evangelists who will be spiritual people, showing consistency in all aspects of their lives, making the most of every opportunity to proclaim Christ crucified to individuals and crowds in all types of settings. Enable the church to encourage young people to devote their lives to this great work. I pray in Jesus' name. Amen.

My personal prayer:

....

....

....

....

....

....

Week 32

Psalm 126:5-6

*T*hose who sow in tears shall reap in joy. He who con-
tinually goes forth weeping, bearing seed for sowing,
shall doubtless come again with rejoicing, bringing his
sheaves with him.

Ruth 2:2-3, 15-17

*S*o Ruth the Moabitess said to Naomi, 'Please let me
go to the field, and glean heads of grain after him in
whose sight I may find favour.' And she said to her, 'Go,
my daughter.' Then she left, and went and gleaned in
the field after the reapers. And she happened to come to
the part of the field belonging to Boaz, who was of the
family of Elimelech. ... And when she rose up to glean,
Boaz commanded his young men, saying, 'Let her glean
even among the sheaves, and do not reproach her. Also let
grain from the bundles fall purposely for her; leave it that
she may glean, and do not rebuke her.' So she gleaned in
the field until evening, and beat out what she had gleaned,
and it was about an ephah of barley.

Meditation

There is a beautiful picture of Ruth gleaning in the fields of Boaz, which though not directly speaking of evangelism is an illustration of the task of personal work. God had given instructions that grain must be left in the corners of the fields for strangers to find sufficient for their needs. The reaper can be careless about odd pieces of wheat, but every one is precious to the gleaner. You can reap with your eyes shut, but the gleaner has to carefully look for each piece of grain which is to be picked up. Humility characterises the gleaner as he or she has to stoop to pick up each piece. But gleaning is effective work: each stalk helps to make a bundle. I have no doubt that God who gave instructions to landowners to leave some produce for the stranger is also careful to ensure that there are 'handfuls of purpose' for us. In other words there are people whom only we can reach with the gospel, so we will want to be careful in looking for opportunities which God is creating for us.

God's harvest field is great,
His labourers are few;
The Master stands before the gate,
He calls for me and you!

> *Lord, here I am, send me!*
> *Help me to win one soul!*
> *From doubts and fears now set me free,*
> *Touch me with Love's live coal.*

He cries, 'Whom shall I send?
Oh, who for Us will go?
Oh, who My wanderers will tend,
Save them from endless woe?'

When all the souls are won,
And gathered in each sheaf,
How thrilled we'll be with Your 'Well done!'
When end life's battles brief.
— COMMISSIONER BOOTH-TUCKER

Prayer

Lord Jesus, It amazes me that You would use even me! For such an overwhelming privilege, I thank and praise You. It fills me with adoration for Your wonderful grace. Whether in sowing, gleaning or reaping, help me to be faithful, and give all the glory back to You. What a wonderful master You are. Help me to be a trustworthy servant. Amen.

My personal prayer:

....

....

....

....

....

....

Week 33

John 1:40-42

One of the two who heard John [the Baptist] speak, and followed Him [Jesus], was Andrew, Simon Peter's brother. He first found his own brother Simon, and said to him, 'We have found the Messiah' (which is translated the Christ). And he brought him to Jesus. He said, 'You are Simon the son of Jonah. You shall be called Cephas' (which is translated, a Stone).

Meditation

Andrew had been a follower of John the Baptist, but when he and fellow disciple, John, heard the Baptist point people to Jesus, the Lamb of God, they left all to follow Him. Then we read that Andrew first found his family. Simon Peter and Andrew were brothers, who no doubt, as boys, had played together, and as young men had worked in the fishing trade. They would have discussed religion, but Andrew was keen to introduce his brother to Jesus. Sharing Christ with one's family is often tough and challenging, and though some times the family can bring great opposition, with love and patience, it may be that the family will be a source of great joy, if God uses us to bring them to faith in Christ.

Lead me to some soul today
Oh, teach me Lord just what to say;
Friends of mine are lost in sin,
And cannot find the way.
Few there are who seem to care,
And few there are who pray.
Melt my heart, and fill my life
To win some soul today.

— WILLIAM HENRY HOUGHTON

Prayer

O God, You are Father, Son and Holy Spirit. You are relational, and You put the solitary in families. Thank you for those who have loved me, and who do love me. I earnestly pray that in Your grace and kindness, You will work in each of their hearts, to make them aware of their need for forgiveness, and reconciliation with You. May I be a faithful witness for You, showing love, respect and honour, trusting You for prompting when to speak and when to keep silent. I pray for Your honour's sake. Amen.

My personal prayer:

....

....

....

....

....

....

Week 34

Mark 2:1-5

*A*nd again [Jesus] entered Capernaum after some days, and it was heard that He was in the house. Immediately many gathered together, so that there was no longer room to receive them, not even near the door. And He preached the word to them. Then they came to Him, bringing a paralytic who was carried by four men.

And when they could not come near Him because of the crowd, they uncovered the roof where He was. So when they had broken through, they let down the bed on which the paralytic was lying. And Jesus saw their faith, He said to the paralytic, 'Son, your sins are forgiven you.'

Meditation

The greatest act of friendship is to introduce someone to Jesus Christ. In Christ, there is reconciliation to God, forgiveness, new life and blessings untold. To keep silent when people need to hear the gospel seems sinful and selfish. It is not sufficient to argue that we witness with deeds, and not words. Time and again we read that Jesus opened His mouth and began to speak, and so should we. To bring people to Jesus takes persistence and faith.

We will want to be winsome, endearing and kind, but we also need to be bold and courageous, not afraid of the reaction of the unsympathetic, but looking for the smile of God on our determination to bring people to Jesus.

꧁꧂

There's a work for Jesus
Ready at your hand,
'Tis a task the Master
Just for you has planned;
Haste to do His bidding,
Yield Him service true;
There's a work for Jesus
None but you can do.

> *Work for Jesus, day by day,*
> *Serve Him ever, falter never; Christ obey,*
> *Yield Him service loyal, true*
> *There's a work for Jesus none but you can do.*

There's a work for Jesus,
Humble tho' it be,
'Tis the very service
He would ask of thee,
Go where fields are whitened,
And the labourers few
There's a work for Jesus
None but you can do.

There's a work for Jesus,
Precious souls to bring,
Tell them of His mercies

Tell them of your King.
Faint not, grow not weary,
He will strength renew;
There's a work for Jesus
None but you can do.

— ELSIE DUNCAN YALE

Prayer

Gracious God and Heavenly Father, I desire that I would be used in the great work of bringing men and women to the Lord Jesus, so that they would find His grace, guidance and gladness, His eternal life. I do not expect this to be easy, but it is Your work and therefore I ask for Your compassionate heart and Your persistent strength to be involved in the task of winning people for Jesus. Amen.

My personal prayer:

....

....

....

....

....

....

Week 35

Mark 4:26-29

*A*nd He said, 'The kingdom of God is as if a man should scatter seed on the ground, and should sleep by night and rise by day, and the seed should sprout and grow, he himself does not know how. For the earth yields crops by itself: first the blade, then the head, after that the full grain in the head. But when the grain ripens, immediately he puts in the sickle, because the harvest has come.'

Meditation

I have a note next to this passage, in the margin of my Bible drawing three conclusions:

1. I can leave the work to God when I have done my duty.
2. I may leave the work to God when He has pledged to do what I cannot.
3. I must leave the work to God, because I do not understand the process.

Stuart Olyott says, 'Almost all mistakes in Christian work are caused by impatience.' Let me work hard, and then leave the rest to God. God's Word does not return to Him void and useless; it has a purpose and that will be accomplished. Remember what happened when young King Josiah discovered the Word? A revival followed. Who knows how God will use His Word today!

I'm not ashamed to own my Lord,
Or to defend His cause;
Maintain the honour of His Word,
The glory of His cross.

Jesus, my God! I know His name,
His name is all my trust;
Nor will He put my soul to shame,
Nor let my hope be lost.

Firm as His throne His promise stands,
And He can well secure
What I've committed to His hands
Till the decisive hour.

Then will He own my worthless name
Before His Father's face;
And in the new Jerusalem
Appoint my soul a place.

— ISAAC WATTS

Prayer

Eternal Heavenly Father, I thank You that You are bigger than and beyond time. I know that You are always in a hurry to save, and indeed to strengthen Your people. But thank you for Your patience and grace. I want to be 'out of breath pursuing souls'[1]

1. This phrase was used to describe Wesley's evangelists in the eighteenth century.

but I also want to be in tune with You, resting in and relying on Your Holy Spirit to do His work in the hearts of those for whom I am praying and to whom I am witnessing. Help me to do my part, and thank you that You will be doing Your part in bringing people to faith. Amen.

My personal prayer:

....

....

....

....

....

....

The Characteristics of Soul Winners

Week 36

Psalm 51:1,12-15

*H*ave mercy upon me, O God, according to Your lovingkindness; according to the multitude of Your tender mercies, blot out my transgressions ... Restore to me the joy of Your salvation, and uphold me by Your generous Spirit. Then I will teach transgressors Your ways, and sinners shall be converted to You. Deliver me from the guilt of bloodshed, O God, the God of my salvation, and my tongue shall sing aloud of Your righteousness. O Lord, open my lips, and my mouth shall show forth Your praise.

Meditation

Despite King David's adultery with Bathsheba and as-good-as murder of Uriah the Hittite, he looked to God for forgiveness and a new start. The Scottish preacher of over a century ago, Alexander Whyte, used to say, 'The Christian life is a series of new beginnings.' Past failures and previous sins, serious though they are, should not keep us from present obedience. Jesus made it clear that our lives should demonstrate, to all around us, what the Lord has done for and in us. But the bottom line is not 'See how good I am!' but 'Christ Jesus came into the world to save sinners … and you and I qualify!' If people find fault in us, then they have pointed out why we need a Saviour. Satan accuses us to keep us from talking about Jesus; the Holy Spirit convicts us, so that we will recognize that our sufficiency is of God, and therefore need not hesitate to share the gospel, even with those who know us best.

For God so loved this sinful world,
His Son He freely gave,
That whosoever would believe,
Eternal life should have.

> *'Tis true, Oh, yes, 'tis true …*
> *God's wonderful promise is true …*
> *For I've trusted, and tested, and tried it,*
> *And I know God's promise is true.*

I was a wayward, wandering child,
A slave to sin and fear,
Until this blessed promise fell
Like music on my ear.

The 'whosoever' of the Lord,
I trusted was for me;
I took Him at His gracious word,
From sin to set me free.

Eternal life begun below
Now fills my heart and soul:
I'll sing His praise for evermore,
Who has redeemed my soul.

— Leila Naylor Morris

Prayer

Lord, You know all about me. You know my sins: the ones I regret, and the ones I sometimes relish; the ones I remember, the ones I have forgotten, and the ones I wish I could forget; the ones of yesterday, today and tomorrow. Who am I to speak for You? Please wash me afresh from all sin, and fill me again with Your Holy Spirit, Your Spirit of holiness. May I this day speak of Jesus and live for Him, in such a way that people see Him only, and find themselves hungry for Him, and homesick for God. I pray in His precious name. Amen.

My personal prayer:

....

....

....

....

....

....

Week 37
1 Thessalonians 2:1-8

For you yourselves know, brethren, that our coming to you was not in vain. But even after we had suffered before and were spitefully treated at Philippi, as you know, we were bold in our God to speak to you the gospel of God in much conflict. For our exhortation did not come from error or uncleanness, nor was it in deceit. But as we have been approved by God to be entrusted with the gospel, even so we speak, not as pleasing men, but God who tests our hearts. For neither at any time did we use flattering words, as you know, nor a cloak for covetousness—God is witness. Nor did we seek glory from men, either from you or from others, when we might have made demands as apostles of Christ. But we were gentle among you, just as a nursing mother cherishes her own children. So, affectionately longing for you, we were well pleased to impart to you not only the gospel of God, but also our own lives, because you had become dear to us.

Proverbs 11:30

The fruit of the righteous is a tree of life, and he who wins souls is wise.

Meditation

There are times when God reveals Himself in spectacular ways—many Muslims are converted having had a dream of Jesus. That is wonderful, but normally people come to Christ having been prayed for and witnessed to over a period of time. Then, maybe at an evangelistic event, they are converted. We need always to be ready to answer the question, 'What must I do to be saved?' And whatever may be pressing, nothing is more urgent than to answer that question. God uses a life characterised by godliness and integrity. Christ-likeness is a fearful weapon in God's hands to reach the lost. So let us pray for consistency in our walk, likeness to Jesus in our work, and fruitfulness in our witness.

Ready to suffer grief or pain,
Ready to stand the test;
Ready to stay at home and send
Others, if He sees best.

> *Ready to go, ready to stay,*
> *Ready my place to fill;*
> *Ready for service, lowly or great,*
> *Ready to do His will.*

Ready to go, ready to bear,
Ready to watch and pray;
Ready to stand aside and give,
Till He shall clear the way.

Ready to speak, ready to think,
Ready with heart and brain;
Ready to stand where He sees fit,
Ready to stand the strain.

> Ready to speak, ready to warn,
> Ready o'er souls to yearn;
> Ready in life, ready in death,
> Ready for His return.

> — CHARLIE D. TILLMAN

Prayer

Heavenly Father, Thank you for the great plan of salvation planned before time began. I praise and worship You for sending the Lord Jesus to die and then to conquer death by rising again. I rejoice that the Holy Spirit has worked in my heart not only to draw me to Yourself, but to make me more like You. I commit myself afresh, asking that you will take and make me a willing servant in Your royal service. I am willing to go anywhere, and do anything for Your glory. Amen.

My personal prayer:

....

....

....

....

....

....

Week 38

1 Thessalonians 2:9-13

*F*or you remember, brethren, our labour and toil;
for labouring night and day, that we might not be
a burden to any of you, we preached to you the gospel
of God. You are witnesses, and God also, how devoutly
and justly and blamelessly we behaved ourselves among
you who believe; as you know how we exhorted, and
comforted, and charged every one of you, as a father does
his own children, that you would walk worthy of God
who calls you into His own kingdom and glory. For this
reason we also thank God without ceasing, because when
you received the word of God which you heard from us,
you welcomed it not as the word of men, but as it is in
truth, the word of God, which also effectively works in
you who believe.

Meditation

God's love towards us, Jesus' death for us and the
Holy Spirit's work within us to mould us into the
image of Christ, make us increasingly concerned for
men and women. Walking closely with our Triune
God will increase the burden we have for others to

trust Christ as Lord and Saviour. Jesus calls us His friends, but we will regard ourselves as His bond-servants, ready and willing to go where He wants and do what He wants. I have friends, one of whom turned down a place at a leading U.K. university to go to an Islamic university in the Middle East to reach students there with the gospel. Another moved to a tough council estate with the same motive. However, recognising that the Lord has placed us in a variety of work situations is itself a challenge. As workers, we are to be true to our calling, but to see ourselves as witnesses in the work place gives significance to all we do. Our greatest calling is to reflect and reveal Jesus to others. 'Nothing is too precious for Jesus.'[1]

❧

Go, labour on; spend, and be spent,
Your joy to do the Father's will;
It is the way the Master went;
Should not the servant tread it still?

Go, labour on; 'tis not for nought;
Your earthly loss is heavenly gain;
Men heed you, love you, praise you not;
The Master praises: what are men?

Go, labour on, while it is day;
The world's dark night is hastening on;
Speed, speed your work, cast sloth away;
It is not thus that souls are won.

Toil on, faint not, keep watch, and pray;
Be wise the erring soul to win;

---

1. Amy Carmichael.

Go forth into the world's highway,
Compel the wanderer to come in.

Toil on, and in your toil rejoice;
For toil comes rest, for exile home;
Soon shall you hear the Bridegroom's voice,
The midweek night cry, 'Behold, I come!'

— HORATIUS BONAR

Prayer

Heavenly Father, thank you for those who prayed for me, taught me the gospel, and then introduced me to Jesus. Thank you for all the work done that I might hear the good news of Jesus' love. Thank you for my moment of conversion. Thank you for all the saints who through the years have given their lives for the cause of Christ, to spread the kingdom. I am such a debtor to You and then to Your people. May I, in turn, give my life that others might enter into the joy of knowing You, too. Use me, use even me, for Your glory I pray. In Jesus' name. Amen.

My personal prayer:

....

....

....

....

....

....

Week 39

1 Peter 3:13-18

A *nd who is he who will harm you if you become followers of what is good? But even if you should suffer for righteousness' sake, you are blessed. And do not be afraid of their threats, nor be troubled. But sanctify the Lord God in your hearts, and always be ready to give a defence to everyone who asks you a reason for the hope that is in you, with meekness and fear; having a good conscience, that when they defame you as evildoers, those who revile your good conduct in Christ may be ashamed. For it is better, if it is the will of God, to suffer for doing good than for doing evil. For Christ also suffered once for sins, the just for the unjust, that He might bring us to God, being put to death in the flesh but made alive by the Spirit.*

Meditation

We are familiar with the marginalisation of Christianity in our land. Whilst not suffering persecution, pressure can mount, and things can be made very difficult for us to live as consistent followers of Jesus. As an old man, Peter was writing to Christians scattered throughout the world. Some had possibly been converted through his sermon in Jerusalem at Pentecost years earlier. He is warning them of difficulties to come, saying:

We should expect times of persecution.
We should not be afraid of what people may do.
We should keep close to the Lord through all times.
We should live godly lives, with a clear conscience.
We should always be ready to explain our Christian faith.

In other words, we must not be intimidated into silence because of the opposition we may be facing. Rather, we are to seize the moment to explain to those who are bewildered by our willingness to suffer for Jesus' sake, why He is so precious to us.

Close to my Saviour, near would I be,
Ready and willing—speak, Lord, to me
At Thine own bidding, forth would I go,
That souls in darkness Thy love may know.

Use me, Lord Jesus, use even me;
Though all unworthy, thine would I be;
In full surrender, my all I give,
Use me, Lord Jesus, use even me.

Seeking the wand'rer where'er he be,
Seeking to bring him back, Lord, to Thee;
Taking the message sent from above,
Speaking of Jesus and His great love.

Just a weak vessel, trusting in Thee,
Filled with Thy Spirit, Thy pow'r in me;

> Faithfully working from day to day,
> Telling the lost ones Christ is the way.
>
> — C. F. WARREN

Prayer

O God, forgive me when I worry and fear, when I am so explicitly commanded not to. Teach me to live having a good conscience, without being provocative. Help me to be kind at all times, and if I am called to suffer for Jesus' sake, may I learn to rejoice and not be bitter. And help me always to fearlessly speak for Jesus, patiently explaining to all why You mean so much to me. I pray, looking to You for strength. Amen.

My personal prayer:

....

....

....

....

....

....

Week 40

Romans 1:8-17

*F*irst, I thank my God through Jesus Christ for you all, that your faith is spoken of throughout the whole world. For God is my witness, whom I serve with my spirit in the gospel of His Son, that without ceasing I make mention of you always in my prayers, making request if, by some means, now at last I may find a way in the will of God to come to you. For I long to see you, that I may impart to you some spiritual gift, so that you may be established— that is, that I may be encouraged together with you by the mutual faith both of you and me. Now I do not want you to be unaware, brethren, that I often planned to come to you (but was hindered until now), that I might have some fruit among you also, just as among the other Gentiles.

I am a debtor both to Greeks and barbarians, both to wise and unwise. So, as much as is in me, I am ready to preach the gospel to you who are in Rome also. For I am not ashamed of the gospel of Christ, for it is the power of God to salvation for everyone who believes, for the Jew first and also for the Greek. For in it the righteousness of

God is revealed from faith to faith; as it is written, 'The just shall live by faith'.

Meditation

Paul, writing to the church in Rome, which he had not yet personally visited, uses the letter to spell out the gospel message. In these verses he says, *'I am a debtor ...'*, *'I am ready'*, and *'I am not ashamed ...'* Then, Paul describes the gospel as the power of God to salvation. It is not a philosophy to be discussed or an idea to be debated, but a power to be unleashed. Like a small acorn has within it the power to grow into a solid oak tree, the gospel of Jesus is so powerful it can reach and transform the most wayward and rebellious. One of the effects of the Word is that it stops the mouths of those who use their God-given breath to deny their Creator. They listen in awe to what the Lord has done and will do.

Stir me, oh! Stir me, Lord, I care not how,
But stir my heart in passion for the world;
Stir me to give, to go, but most to pray;
Stir, till the gospel banner be unfurled
O'er lands that still in heathen darkness lie,
O'er deserts where no Cross is lifted high.

Stir me, oh! Stir me, Lord, till all my heart
Is filled with strong compassion for these souls;
Till Your compelling Word drives me to pray;
Till Your constraining love reach to the poles
Far north and south, in burning deep desire,
Till east and west are caught in love's great fire.

Stir me, oh! Stir me, Lord, till prayer is pain,
Till prayer is joy, till prayer turns into praise;
Stir me, till heart and will and mind, yea all
Is wholly Yours to use through all the day.
Stir, till I learn to pray exceedingly;
Stir, till I learn to wait expectantly.

Stir me, oh! Stir me, Lord, Your heart was stirred
By love's intensest fire, till You did give
Your only Son, Your best belovèd One,
E'en to the dreadful Cross, that I might live.
Stir me to give myself so back to You,
That You can give Yourself again through me.

Stir me, oh! Stir me, Lord, for I can see
Your glorious triumph-day begin to break;
The dawn already gilds the eastern sky;
O, church of Christ, arise, awake, awake;
Oh! Stir us, Lord, as heralds of that day,
For night is past, our King is on His way.

— Mrs A. Head

Prayer

Lord, prevent me from becoming so familiar with great gospel truths that I forget that it is 'the gospel of God'. Thank you that throughout history lives have been eternally transformed through all that Jesus accomplished by His death and resurrection. Remind me that Jesus is the same yesterday, today and forever, and is still able to save to the uttermost all who come to Him. I praise You that salvation is not through works of righteousness which I have done, but according to Your mercy and grace alone. Amen.

My personal prayer:

....

....

....

....

....

....

Week 41

Isaiah 55:8-11

'F or My thoughts are not your thoughts, Nor are your ways My ways,' says the LORD. 'For as the heavens are higher than the earth, so are My ways higher than your ways, and My thoughts than your thoughts. For as the rain comes down, and the snow from heaven, and do not return there, but water the earth, And make it bring forth and bud, That it may give seed to the sower and bread to the eater, so shall My word be that goes forth from My mouth; It shall not return to Me void, but it shall accomplish what I please, and it shall prosper in the thing for which I sent it.

Meditation

There is a famine in the land, not of food and drink, but of the Word of God. We need to get out the Word, so that people again become familiar with it. Children need to know Bible stories, people need to see Bible texts, everyone needs to possess a Bible, which they read, and churches need to preach and teach the Word of God. What a promise the Lord then gives that His Word will not return void, but will accomplish that for which it was sent. The greatest tragedy is for people to live and die, and not know the Word, not hear the gospel. Could life be more pointless? We were made to know God, and without Him people are lost, barren, hungry, thirsty and rebellious. They need God's Word!

Tell it out among the heathen that the Lord is King!
Tell it out among the nations, bid them shout and sing!
Tell it out with adoration, that He shall increase;
That the mighty King of Glory is the King of Peace
Tell it out with jubilation, though the waves may roar,
That He's seated on the water-floods, our King for
    evermore!

Tell it out among the nations that the Saviour reigns!
Tell it out among the heathen, bid them burst their chains!
Tell it out among the weeping ones that Jesus lives;
Tell it out among the weary ones what rest He gives;
Tell it out among the sinners that He came to save;
Tell it out among the dying that He triumphed o'er the
    grave.

Tell it out among the heathen Jesus reigns above!
Tell it out among the nations that His name is Love!
Tell it out among the highways, and the lanes at home;
Let it ring across the mountains and the ocean foam;
Like the sound of many waters let our glad shout be,
Till it echo and re-echo from the islands of the sea.
— FRANCES RIDLEY HAVERGAL

Prayer

Thank you God that You have spoken, and indeed do still speak. I pray for all those who are getting the Word of God into the hands and hearts of people. Prosper the work of those who distribute Bibles, who display Christian posters, who place Christian children's books in libraries, schools and homes, who give away gospel tracts and who proclaim Your Word. Be merciful to those on the media, in schools and universities, and even in churches who distort Your Word. Bring again, I pray, times of refreshing in my day in this country. In Jesus' name. Amen.

My personal prayer:

....

....

....

....

....

....

Week 42

Acts 28:16-31

*N*ow when we came to Rome, the centurion delivered the prisoners to the captain of the guard; but Paul was permitted to dwell by himself with the soldier who guarded him.

And it came to pass after three days that Paul called the leaders of the Jews together. So when they had come together, he said to them: 'Men and brethren, though I have done nothing against our people or the customs of our fathers, yet I was delivered as a prisoner from Jerusalem into the hands of the Romans, who, when they had examined me, wanted to let me go, because there was no cause for putting me to death. But when the Jews spoke against it, I was compelled to appeal to Caesar, not that I had anything of which to accuse my nation. For this reason therefore I have called for you, to see you and speak with you, because for the hope of Israel I am bound with this chain.'

Then they said to him, 'We neither received letters from Judea concerning you, nor have any of the brethren who came reported or spoken any evil of you. But we desire to hear from you what you think; for concerning this sect, we know that it is spoken against everywhere.'

So when they had appointed him a day, many came to him at his lodging, to whom he explained and solemnly testified of the kingdom of God, persuading them concerning Jesus from both the Law of Moses and the Prophets, from morning till evening. And some were persuaded by the things which were spoken, and some disbelieved. So when they did not agree among themselves, they departed after Paul had said one word: 'The Holy Spirit spoke rightly through Isaiah the prophet to our fathers ...' Then Paul dwelt two whole years in his own rented house, and received all who came to him, preaching the kingdom of God and teaching the things which concern the Lord Jesus Christ with all confidence, no one forbidding him.

Meditation

Paul always wanted to go to Rome to preach the gospel, but he arrived there as a prisoner rather than a preacher! Nevertheless, he quickly devised a strategy to reach people. He didn't go on a pity-party and moan, feeling sorry for himself in prison. Inviting them to his prison—he was under house arrest—he used the Old Testament to point people to Jesus. All the Bible is about Jesus. The Scripture was Paul's authority for all that he said. Notice the three verbs: explained, testified, persuaded. The evangelist will want to explain the gospel, testify to its effectiveness and then persuade the hearer to actually respond to the love and call of Jesus. Paul did this from morning till evening. It was not a hobby, but his all-consuming passion. Here is Paul, an old man, waiting for martyr-dom, and he is evangelising! If the gospel is true, how could he, or we, do anything less?

❦

Give me a passion for souls, dear Lord,
A passion to save the lost;
Oh, that Your love were by all adored,
And welcomed at any cost.

Jesus, I long, I long to be winning
Men who are lost, and constantly sinning;
Oh, may this hour be one of beginning
The story of pardon to tell.

Though there are dangers untold and stern
Confronting me in the way
Willingly still would I go, nor turn,
But trust You for grace each day.

How shall this passion for souls be mine?
Lord, please make the answer clear;
Help me to throw out the old life-Line
To those who are struggling near.

— Herbert G. Tovey

Prayer

Lord, I want to follow Paul as he followed Jesus. May I use the Bible to point people to Jesus. May the Lord Jesus Himself be central in all my witnessing. May I be faithful in proclamation in whatever situation I am found. May I give my whole life to making Jesus known—all my days, and all the hours of each day. Teach me never to give up in the great task of proclaiming Jesus to others, I pray. Amen.

My personal prayer:

....

....

....

....

....

....

Week 43

2 Corinthians 6:3-10

*W*e give no offence in anything, that our ministry may not be blamed. But in all things we commend ourselves as ministers of God: in much patience, in tribulations, in needs, in distresses, in stripes, in imprisonments, in tumults, in labours, in sleeplessness, in fastings; by purity, by knowledge, by longsuffering, by kindness, by the Holy Spirit, by sincere love, by the word of truth, by the power of God, by the armour of righteousness on the right hand and on the left, by honour and dishonour, by evil report and good report; as deceivers, and yet true; as unknown, and yet well known; as dying, and behold we live; as chastened, and yet not killed; as sorrowful, yet always rejoicing; as poor, yet making many rich; as having nothing, and yet possessing all things.*

Meditation

The 150 Psalms can be summarized with the words: Life is tough; but God is good. Paul found exactly the same. He refused to focus on the negatives or the discouragements, but saw that even in the difficulty

God was working out His purposes and doing His work. God has never uttered the words, 'I didn't expect that!' He has never been taken by surprise. He knows what He is doing in our lives. We may not receive honours from the Queen, and may face struggles that others do not understand, but God is at work in and through us, and what could possibly be better than that. If only we could see everything from eternity's point of view, how different would it all appear.

Is your life a channel of blessing?
Is the love of God flowing through you?
Are you telling the lost of the Saviour?
Are you ready His service to do?

> *Make me a channel of blessing today;*
> *Make me a channel of blessing I pray;*
> *My life possessing, my service blessing,*
> *Make me a channel of blessing today.*

Is your life a channel of blessing?
Are you caring for those that are lost?
Have you told of the offered salvation
Christ purchased for them at such cost?

We shall not be channels of blessing
If we consciously trifle with sin;
We shall barriers be and a hindrance
To those we are trying to win.

— HAPER GARCIA SMITH

Prayer

Lord, teach me the truth of :
Only one life; 'twill soon be passed;
only what's done for Jesus will last.
Help me to understand that the things of earth need to grow strangely dim in the light of the glory and grace of Jesus, and eternity. I pray in His holy name. Amen.

My personal prayer:

....

....

....

....

....

....

Week 44

2 Timothy 4:1-5

I charge you therefore before God and the Lord Jesus Christ, who will judge the living and the dead at His appearing and His kingdom: preach the word! Be ready in season and out of season. Convince, rebuke, exhort, with all longsuffering and teaching. For the time will come when they will not endure sound doctrine, but according to their own desires, because they have itching ears, they will heap up for themselves teachers; and they will turn their ears away from the truth, and be turned aside to fables. But you be watchful in all things, endure afflictions, do the work of an evangelist, fulfil your ministry.

Meditation

Paul was writing his final words. He had fought the good fight, finished the race and kept the faith. The baton was passed on to young, timid Timothy who was an able pastor of a church. Timothy was not naturally an evangelist. Every Christian is a witness, and pastors are here encouraged to do the work of an evangelist. God has given evangelists to His church, but all Christians will want to pass on what Jesus means to us and what He wants to do for all people. We must not hide behind the 'I'm not gifted' excuse, or we will lose the great joy of seeing others come to faith through our witness.

❧

Jesus! the Name high over all,
In hell or earth or sky;
Angels and men before it fall,
And devils fear and fly.

Jesus! the Name to sinners dear,
The Name to sinners giv'n;
It scatters all their guilty fear,
It turns their hell to Heav'n.

Jesus! the prisoner's fetters breaks,
And bruises Satan's head;
Power into strengthless souls it speaks,
And life into the dead.

Oh, that the world might taste and see
The riches of His grace!
The arms of love that compass me
Would all the world embrace.

Happy, if with my latest breath
I may but gasp His Name,
Preach Him to all and cry in death,
'Behold, behold the Lamb!'

— CHARLES WESLEY

Prayer

Lord Jesus, Thank you for Your promise to build Your church, and thank you that You Yourself have given gifts to the church. I praise You for church leaders and congregations throughout the world, and specifically for the gift of the evangelist. Please raise up more who will be used to reach the lost and equip the saints for the work of ministry and edification. I am grateful for the gifts that You have given and entrusted to me. Help me to use them for Your glory, and help me too, to do the work of the evangelist through every stage and season of my life. Amen.

My personal prayer:

....

....

....

....

....

....

Suffering

Week 45

Matthew 24:1-14

*T*hen *Jesus went out and departed from the temple,
and His disciples came up to show Him the buildings
of the temple. And Jesus said to them, 'Do you not see
all these things? Assuredly, I say to you, not one stone
shall be left here upon another, that shall not be thrown
down.'*

*Now as He sat on the Mount of Olives, the disciples
came to Him privately, saying, 'Tell us, when will these
things be? And what will be the sign of Your coming, and
of the end of the age?' And Jesus answered and said to
them: 'Take heed that no one deceives you. For many will
come in My name, saying, "I am the Christ," and will
deceive many. And you will hear of wars and rumours of
wars. See that you are not troubled; for all these things
must come to pass, but the end is not yet. For nation
will rise against nation, and kingdom against kingdom.
And there will be famines, pestilences, and earthquakes
in various places. All these are the beginning of sorrows.*

*'Then they will deliver you up to tribulation and kill
you, and you will be hated by all nations for My name's
sake. And then many will be offended, will betray one*

another, and will hate one another. Then many false prophets will rise up and deceive many. And because lawlessness will abound, the love of many will grow cold. But he who endures to the end shall be saved. And this gospel of the kingdom will be preached in all the world as a witness to all the nations, and then the end will come.'

Meditation

There are many signs to look for as the time of the return of the Lord Jesus draws near. One of these will be the widespread proclamation of the gospel. People from every tribe and tongue will be with the Lord praising Him for eternity, but first they will have been reached with the gospel. To reach the lost, to hasten the return of Jesus is our priority. This cause deserves all our resources, our energy, our prayer, our involvement. People who loved not their lives even unto death are especially honoured in glory, but this is our reasonable service after what the Lord has done for us.

Use me, dear Lord, as a channel of blessing,
Fill with Your love, fill with Your love;
To thirsty souls send me forth with a message,
A message from Heaven above.

Cleansed from my sin, emptied of self,
Filled from the fountain of blessing above;
Use me, dear Lord, as a channel of blessing,
A channel to carry Your love.

Make of my life Lord, a channel of blessing,
Thy dwelling place, Thy dwelling place,

Take away all that would hinder Thy Spirit
And then overflow with Thy grace.

Give me a heart sympathetic and tender,
Jesus like Yours, Jesus like Yours;
Touched by the needs that are surging around me
And filled with compassion divine.

— MARTHA S. CLINGAN

Prayer

Lord, why do I struggle to give You everything? Forgive me! The Lord Jesus fully gave Himself for me. Afresh, I willingly submit to Your Lordship, Your Kingly reign in my life. I want to hold nothing back. I turn my back on my own selfish way, and want to follow You. I take up my cross, and die to all that would tie me to this world. I deny myself, but only ask that I might be helped to exalt Jesus in all I do and say. Amen.

My personal prayer:

....

....

....

....

....

....

Week 46

Matthew 13:24-31, 36-43

A nother parable He put forth to them, saying: 'The kingdom of heaven is like a man who sowed good seed in his field; but while men slept, his enemy came and sowed tares among the wheat and went his way. But when the grain had sprouted and produced a crop, then the tares also appeared. So the servants of the owner came and said to him, "Sir, did you not sow good seed in your field? How then does it have tares?" He said to them, "An enemy has done this." The servants said to him, "Do you want us then to go and gather them up?" But he said, "No, lest while you gather up the tares you also uproot the wheat with them. Let both grow together until the harvest, and at the time of harvest I will say to the reapers, 'First gather together the tares and bind them in bundles to burn them, but gather the wheat into my barn.' "*

...Then Jesus sent the multitude away and went into the house. And His disciples came to Him, saying, 'Explain to us the parable of the tares of the field.'

He answered and said to them: 'He who sows the good seed is the Son of Man. The field is the world, the good seeds are the sons of the kingdom, but the tares are the sons of the wicked one. The enemy who sowed them is the devil, the harvest is the end of the age, and the reapers are the angels. Therefore as the tares are gathered and burned in the fire, so it will be at the end of this age. The Son of Man will send out His angels, and they will gather out of His kingdom all things that offend, and those who practice lawlessness, and will cast them into the furnace of fire. There will be wailing and gnashing of teeth. Then the righteous will shine forth as the sun in the kingdom of their Father. He who has ears to hear, let him hear!'

Meditation

The biggest disappointment in my Christian life is to have seen a lack of integrity in 'Christian' people. I am amazed how inconsistent have been the lives of some professing believers. But this passage gives me every right to wonder whether they may not be Christians at all. We all fail; we all sin, but a real believer cannot live comfortably when bearing a grudge, when disobeying a command, while living inconsistently. Having a relationship with God will impact us twenty four hours a day: at work, at home as well as at church. Until the second coming of Christ, believers will always be living alongside unbelievers, and sometimes it may not be easy to differentiate which is which. The harvest is the end of the world, and then the separation will be final. Telling others, confirms the message in our own hearts. Let us remind ourselves of the gospel each day, and make sure that we are amongst the wheat and not the weeds.

❧

Jesus, Thy blood and righteousness
My beauty are, my glorious dress;
'Midst flaming worlds, in these arrayed,
With joy shall I lift up my head.
Bold shall I stand in that great day,
For who aught to my charge shall lay?

Lord, I believe Thy precious blood,
Which at the Mercy Seat of God
For ever doth for sinners plead,
For me, even for my soul was shed.
Fully absolved through these I am
From sin and fear, from guilt and shame.

Oh! Give to all Thy servants, Lord,
With power to speak, Thy gracious Word.
That all who to Thy wounds will flee
May find eternal life in Thee.
Thou God of power, Thou God of love,
Let the whole world Thy mercy prove.

— COUNT VON ZINZENDORF

Prayer

Lord, You are the Judge of all. Thank you that my righteousness is not worked for, but received. Thank you that who I am in Christ is all His doing, and not mine. Thank you that You have made me Yours, not for the years of time alone, but for all eternity. Thank you that I have been saved not by works of righteousness that I have done, but according to Your mercy. Make me bold to tell others that by grace they are saved, through faith, and that not of themselves, but that it is the gift of God. Amen.

My personal prayer:

....

....

....

....

....

....

Week 47

2 Timothy 2:7-12

*F*or God has not given us a spirit of fear, but of power
and of love and of a sound mind. Therefore do not
be ashamed of the testimony of our Lord, nor of me His
prisoner, but share with me in the sufferings for the
gospel according to the power of God, who has saved
us and called us with a holy calling, not according to
our works, but according to His own purpose and grace
which was given us in Christ Jesus ... For this reason
I suffer these things ...

Colossians 4:18

*R*emember those in chains.

Meditation

We owe it to all our brothers and sisters in Christ
who have suffered in the past to read *Foxes Book of
Martyrs*[1] and to remember with thanksgiving those
who have stood firm for the faith. At least seven
times the Apostle Paul wrote to others and asked for
prayer for himself. In Colossians he says we should
pray for those who currently were/are in chains

---

1. Or for a younger generation *Jesus Freaks* is very powerful too.

for the sake of the gospel. The Lord Jesus and New Testament writers warned us that suffering is part of the Christian life. Hebrews 11:32-38 recalls specific persecution, and similar atrocities continue today. Christians and congregations, especially in the comfortable West, must regularly pray for these dear believers who suffer for Christ, and who witness for Him in what they are enduring, and indeed saying.

༺❀༻

Jesus, and shall it ever be
A mortal man ashamed of Thee,
Ashamed of Thee, whom angels praise,
Whose glories shine through endless days?

Ashamed of Jesus, of my God,
Who purchased me with His own blood!
Of Him who, to retrieve my loss
Despised the shame, endured the cross?

Ashamed of Jesus, that dear Friend,
On whom my hopes of heaven depend!
No, when I blush, be this my shame,
That I no more revere His name.

Ashamed of Jesus! Yes, I may
When I've no guilt to wash away,
No tear to wipe, no good to crave,
No fears to quell, no soul to save.

Ashamed of Jesus, of my Lord,
By all heaven's glorious hosts adored!
No, I will make my boast of Thee,
In time and in eternity!

Till then, nor is my boasting vain,
Till then I boast a Saviour slain!
And Oh, may this my glory be,
That Christ is not ashamed of me!
— JOSEPH GRIGG AND BENJAMIN FRANCIS

Prayer

Loving Heavenly Father, I recognise that You never waste any pain or sorrow. I know too, that Your dear Son, suffered that I and millions of others might be saved. But O God, when I read what Your children are enduring, my heart goes out to them. I earnestly pray for such. Make them bold, loving, courageous, strong in faith and endurance. Help them to be Christ-like to their captors and persecutors. If they are to be martyred, may they experience Your close presence in the shadow of death. If they are to continue in their suffering, help them to rejoice and be exceedingly glad, knowing that their reward in heaven is great. If they are to be delivered, keep them faithful, fearing not the ones who can only destroy the body, but You who have their eternal destiny in Your hand. May I be willing, if need be, to suffer for righteousness' sake, not being afraid of people's threats nor being troubled. I pray in the name of Jesus. Amen.

My personal prayer:

....

....

....

....

....

....

Children and Families

Week 48

1 Corinthians 7:10-14

To the married I give this command (not I, but the Lord): a wife must not separate from her husband. But if she does, she must remain unmarried or else be reconciled to her husband. And a husband must not divorce his wife.

To the rest I say this (I, not the Lord): if any brother has a wife who is not a believer and she is willing to live with him, he must not divorce her. And if a woman has a husband who is not a believer and he is willing to live with her, she must not divorce him. For the unbelieving husband has been sanctified through his wife, and the unbelieving wife has been sanctified through her believing husband. Otherwise your children would be unclean, but as it is, they are holy.

Meditation

This passage is not an easy one to either understand or accept. There are many Christians living in homes where their nearest and dearest are unconverted. For some this can be like drinking an ocean-full of sorrow teaspoon by teaspoon. For others, there is the daily grief of seeing close relatives waste their life which is lived in rebellion to the Word of God. Our heart's desire and prayer is that he or she may be saved. God uses the bitter experience to teach us to grieve over the things which grieve Him, as well as to learn patience. Whilst the Bible does not promise that the one we long for will be converted, there is a strong hint that with love and prayer, they will come through to the Lord.

Kind souls who for the miseries moan
Of those who seldom mind their own,
But treat your zeal with cold disdain,
Resolved to make your labours vain;

You whose sincere affection tends
To help your dear ungrateful friends.
That think you foes, or mad, or fools
Because you fain would save their souls;

Though deaf to every warning given,
They scorn to walk with you to heaven,
But often think and sometimes say
They'll never go if that's the way.

Though they the Spirit of God resist,
Or ridicule your faith in Christ;
Though they blaspheme, oppose, condemn
And hate you for your love of them,

One secret way is left you still
To do them good against their will;
Here they can no obstruction give
You may do this without their leave.

Fly to the throne of grace by prayer
And pour out all your wishes there;
Effectual fervent prayer prevails
Where every other method fails.

— JOSEPH HART

Prayer

O gracious God, You understand all things. Hear my prayer for the one I so love and long to be saved. And for those I know who are in this same situation, please grant their desire to see their whole household coming to the knowledge of You. Help me to live lovingly and consistently, so that those near me may see my good works and glorify You. But when I fail, help me to remember that You are the Saviour of sinners, and that is why I need You! Lord, I look to You in my need, and cry to You for help. Amen.

My personal prayer:

....

....

....

....

....

....

Week 49

Matthew 18:1-5, 10-14

A *t that time the disciples came to Jesus, saying, 'Who*
then is greatest in the kingdom of heaven?' Then
Jesus called a little child to Him, set him in the midst of
them, and said, 'Assuredly, I say to you, unless you are
converted and become as little children, you will by no
means enter the kingdom of heaven. Therefore whoever
humbles himself as this little child is the greatest in the
kingdom of heaven. Whoever receives one little child like
this in My name receives Me.

... 'Take heed that you do not despise one of these little
ones, for I say to you that in heaven their angels always
see the face of My Father who is in heaven. For the Son of
Man has come to save that which was lost. What do you
think? If a man has a hundred sheep, and one of them
goes astray, does he not leave the ninety-nine and go to
the mountains to seek the one that is straying? And if he
should find it, assuredly, I say to you, he rejoices more
over that sheep than over the ninety-nine that did not go
astray. Even so it is not the will of your Father who is in
heaven that one of these little ones should perish.'

Meditation

The hymn is hardly modern. Nevertheless there is a truth here which though expressed quaintly mustn't be forgotten. Zechariah reminds us that in the New Jerusalem there is the sound of little children playing in the streets. God has little children on His heart. They are precious to Him. Jesus said that He wanted the children to come to Him, adding 'For of such is the kingdom of God.' The United Nations has a wonderful list of the rights of a child. But in addition, surely every child has the right to be prayed for, and to hear the story of Jesus and His love. Sadly, around us are children for whom nobody prays. Children who don't have a connection with church, who do not have a Christian school teacher, without godly parents, may never have anyone to pray for them. When Hannah gave birth to Samuel, she said, 'For this child I prayed, and the Lord heard my prayer and granted my request.' Perhaps today you could start praying for an un-prayed-for-child to make him or her somebody who is regularly brought before the Lord in prayer.

When mothers of Salem their children brought to Jesus,
The stern disciples drove them back and bade them
    to depart:
But Jesus saw them ere they fled and sweetly smiled and
    kindly said,
'Suffer little children to come unto Me.

For I will receive them and fold them to My bosom:
I'll be a shepherd to these lambs, Oh, drive them not away;
For if their hearts to Me they give, they shall with Me in
    glory live:
Suffer little children to come unto Me.'

How kind was our Saviour to bid these children welcome!
But there are many thousands who have never heard
    His Name;
The Bible they have never read, they know not that the
    Saviour said,
'Suffer little children to come unto Me.'

Oh, soon may the heathen of every tribe and nation
Fulfil Thy blessèd Word and cast their idols all away!
Oh, shine upon them from above and show Thyself a
    God of love,
Teach the little children to come unto Thee!

— WILLIAM MEDLEN HUTCHINGS

Prayer

Heavenly Father, I am living in a society where children are abused physically, emotionally, intellectually and spiritually. Oh, how it must hurt Your loving heart. Jesus is the Friend of little children, so I pray that He will be a friend to the boys and girls of today's society. Keep them from physical, emotional, intellectual and spiritual evil. May they hear about the Lord Jesus in such a way that they will want to trust Him, follow Him, and grow to love Him. Amen.

My personal prayer:

....
....
....
....
....
....

Week 50

Luke 15:11-32

*T*hen He said: 'A certain man had two sons. And the younger of them said to his father, "Father, give me the portion of goods that falls to me." So he divided to them his livelihood. And not many days after, the younger son gathered all together, journeyed to a far country, and there wasted his possessions with prodigal living. But when he had spent all, there arose a severe famine in that land, and he began to be in want. Then he went and joined himself to a citizen of that country, and he sent him into his fields to feed swine. And he would gladly have filled his stomach with the pods that the swine ate, and no one gave him anything. But when he came to himself, he said, "How many of my father's hired servants have bread enough and to spare, and I perish with hunger! I will arise and go to my father, and will say to him, 'Father, I have sinned against heaven and before you, and I am no longer worthy to be called your son. Make me like one of your hired servants.'" And he arose and came to his father. But when he was still a great way off, his father saw him and had compassion,* *and ran and fell on his neck and kissed him. And the son said to him, "Father, I have sinned against heaven and in your sight, and am no longer worthy to be called your son." But the father said to his servants, "Bring out the best robe and put it on him, and put a ring on his hand and sandals on his feet. And bring the fatted calf here and kill it, and let us eat and be merry; for this my son was dead and is alive again; he was lost and is found." And they began to be merry.'*

Meditation

How many hundreds of thousands of Christian parents have gone through the immense sadness of seeing their beloved children become either prodigal or pharisaical. Is there anything more heartbreaking than watching one's children becoming wayward? Foolishness is bound up in the heart of all children, but we can pray that through God's grace, and godly parenting and influences, the children will truly repent and believe. I am sure that there should be more prayer in our church prayer meetings for our children. And also, every parent who prays will surely pray that God will put a hedge around their children and do the miracle of bringing them to saving faith in Christ.

Confirm, O Lord, that word of Thine,
That heavenly word of certainty,
Thou gavest it: I made it mine,
Believed to see.

And yet I see not; he, for whom
That good word came in Thy great love,
Is wandering still, and there is room
For fear to move.

O God of Hope, what though afar
From all desire that wanderer seems
Thy promise fails not; never are
Thy comforts dreams.

— AMY CARMICHAEL

Prayer

God of all grace, I earnestly pray for the children that are particularly close to my heart, and for whom I have special responsibility. Above all else, please save them; please bring them to know You in a deep and real way. Keep them from having second-hand, pass-me-on religion. I long for their gifts and talents to be developed, and then used to honour You. Help me to lovingly, patiently fulfil my responsibilities to them, but give me the joy of seeing them walking with You. I pray for Your glory alone. Amen.

My personal prayer:

....

....

....

....

....

....

Conclusion

Week 51

Daniel 12:1-3

*A*t *that time Michael shall stand up, the great prince who stands watch over the sons of your people; and there shall be a time of trouble, such as never was since there was a nation, even to that time. And at that time your people shall be delivered, every one who is found written in the book. And many of those who sleep in the dust of the earth shall awake, some to everlasting life, some to shame and everlasting contempt. Those who are wise shall shine like the brightness of the firmament, and those who turn many to righteousness like the stars forever and ever.*

Meditation

It is hard to imagine any greater honour than to have a statue of oneself put in a town centre, or in a park, or parliament! Most of us will not even have our lives written up in the obituary columns of the newspaper. Randolf Churchill, son of Sir Winston, said the only time he would hit the headlines would be when he died. Unfortunately, he died on the day Robert Kennedy was assassinated, so even then Randolf was only a column inch or two in the inside pages of the papers! But so what! In time, we will all be forgotten as far as earth is concerned. Look again at that last sentence in the quotation from Daniel. Is anything more significant than having God's smile on our service; His blessing on our lives? And then to have the thrill of knowing that the Lord used us to rescue some dear person from the brink of hell, and for them to enjoy eternity in God's glorious presence. My life takes on real meaning not by seeking the praise of men and women, but by serving the Lord of all glory.

Where He leads me I will follow,
Over land or on the sea.
Where He leads me I will follow,
For He's done so much for me.
Millions still are lost and dying,
They are doomed and cannot see.
Can we let them die without Him,
When we have the message free?

Jesus left His home in Glory
For the cross of Calvary;
How can I do less than serve Him,
Since He's done so much for me?
Here's my life, Lord, fill me, use me,
Help me win the lost to Thee.
Where you lead I will follow,
For you've done so much for me.

As we labour in Christ Jesus
Standing firm and true to Him.
He will help us to win others,
That the light may not grow dim.
So we onward go, not knowing

Ought of that which lies ahead,
Save that as we labour faithfully,
By Christ Jesus we are led.
— ALVIN A. RASMUSSEN

Prayer

O God, You are eternal, and all that You do is protected from the ravages of time. Your thoughts are not my thoughts, and Your ways are not the ways of this fallen world. I want, with John the Baptist, to see Your Name increase, and for me to decrease. Adjust my thinking that I may invest my life in that which will outlast time and be of consequence eternally. Help me to lay hold on eternal life. As the chorus says, 'Here I am, wholly available.' Use me in the great task of bringing people to the Lord Jesus, and loving them for His sake. Keep me from trifling my life away, but rather to be doing only what You would have me do. And I will be careful to give You all the glory. Amen.

My personal prayer:

....

....

....

....

....

....

Week 52

Revelation 7:9-12

*A*fter these things I looked, and behold, a great multitude which no one could number, of all nations, tribes, peoples, and tongues, standing before the throne and before the Lamb, clothed with white robes, with palm branches in their hands, and crying out with a loud voice, saying, 'Salvation belongs to our God who sits on the throne, and to the Lamb!' All the angels stood around the throne and the elders and the four living creatures, and fell on their faces before the throne and worshipped God, saying: 'Amen! Blessing and glory and wisdom, thanksgiving and honour and power and might, be to our God forever and ever. Amen.'

Meditation

In the early chapters of Revelation we read the songs of heaven. First there is praise for creation, then there is praise for redemption, and here there is praise for Jesus, the Lamb who was slain. Considering all that Jesus has done, I want to add the personal pronoun 'My' before each of the nouns in 'Blessing and glory and wisdom, thanksgiving and honour and power and might'. What I have may not be much, but I want it all to be given to Jesus. And whatever I give to Jesus, He gave me in the first place! Then, as with the loaves and fishes, he takes my meagre offering, blesses it and multiplies it to bless others. This is life's greatest investment.

We have heard the joyful sound;
Jesus saves!
Spread the tidings all around:
Jesus saves!
Bear the news to every land,
Climb the steeps and cross the waves.
Onward! 'tis our Lord's command:
Jesus saves!

Sing above the battle's strife:
Jesus saves!
By His death and endless life,
Jesus saves!
Sing it softly through the gloom,
When the heart for mercy craves
Sing in triumph o'er the tomb:
Jesus saves!

Give the winds a mighty voice:
Jesus saves!
Let the nations now rejoice:
Jesus saves!
Shout salvation full and free,
Highest hills and deepest caves;
This our song of victory:
Jesus saves!

— PRISCILLA JANE OWENS

Prayer

Thank you, Creator God, for the wonder of the world in which I live; for its beauty, its order, its variety, I praise You. Thank you, Lord Jesus, for the work of redemption You accomplished at such great cost on the cross, in the tomb, and by rising from the dead. And thank you for the Holy Spirit, who gave me new life and has implanted within me a desire to worship You. Oh, I cry to You for those who know nothing of this love. Be merciful to them, who may also see that salvation belongs to the Lord. Amen.

My personal prayer:

....

....

....

....

....

....

My Prayer Book
Special praise and thanksgiving

Daily prayer requests
Family

....

....

....

....

....

....

....

Special friends

....

....

....

....

....

....

....

Christians with whom I am particularly linked

....

....

....

....

....

....

....

Churches and ministry work particularly close to my heart

....

....

....

....

....

....

....

My prayer requests for myself

....

....

....

....

....

....

....

Intensive prayer unit

....

....

....

....

....

....

....

Urgent prayer requests

....

....

....

....

....

....

....

Sunday, the Lord's Day
Church leaders, pastors and ministers

....

....

....

....

....

....

....

Monday
Missionaries

....

....

....

....

....

....

....

Needy nations of the world

....

....

....

....

....

....

....

Tuesday
Those working with students

....

....

....

....

....

....

....

Those working with children

....
....
....
....
....
....
....

Summer camps and beach missions

....
....
....
....
....
....
....

Those distributing Bibles, Christian books and tracts

....
....
....
....
....
....
....

Wednesday
Evangelists working nearer home

....
....
....
....
....
....
....

My national and local government; the media, and schools

....
....
....
....
....
....
....

Thursday
Churches I know, and their leaders

....
....
....
....
....
....
....

Other ministries and their leaders

....
....
....
....
....
....
....

Friday
Children for whom no one else is praying

....
....
....
....
....
....
....

Children who live on my street

....
....
....
....
....
....
....

Children who are relatives of mine

....

....

....

....

....

....

....

My local schools, and Christians who teach in them

....

....

....

....

....

....

....

Saturday
My unconverted friends and colleagues

....

....

....

....

....

....

....

Christians who have lost their way

....

....

....

....

....

....

....

Christians who are undergoing battles and temptations

....

....

....

....

....

....

....

Other Christian friends

....

....

....

....

....

....

....

Occasional prayer requests

....

....

....

....

....

....

....

TRUTHFORLIFE®

THE BIBLE-TEACHING MINISTRY OF **ALISTAIR BEGG**

The mission of Truth For Life is to teach the Bible with clarity and relevance so that unbelievers will be converted, believers will be established, and local churches will be strengthened.

Daily Program

Each day, Truth For Life distributes the Bible teaching of Alistair Begg across the U.S. and in several locations outside of the U.S. through 1,800 radio outlets. To find a radio station near you, visit **truthforlife.org/stationfinder**.

Free Teaching

The daily program, and Truth For Life's entire teaching archive of over 2,000 Bible-teaching messages, can be accessed for free online and through Truth For Life's full-feature mobile app. Download the free mobile app at **truthforlife.org/app** and listen free online at **truthforlife.org**.

At-Cost Resources

Books and full-length teaching from Alistair Begg on CD, DVD, and USB are available for purchase at cost, with no markup. Visit **truthforlife.org/store**.

Where to Begin?

If you're new to Truth For Life and would like to know where to begin listening and learning, find starting point suggestions at **truthforlife.org/firststep**. For a full list of ways to connect with Truth For Life, visit **truthforlife.org/subscribe**.

Contact Truth For Life

P.O. Box 398000 Cleveland, Ohio 44139
phone 1 (888) 588-7884   **email** letters@truthforlife.org
 /truthforlife @truthforlife **truthforlife.org**

ROGER CARSWELL

AND SOME EVANGELISTS

Growing Your Church Through Discovering
and Developing Evangelists

And Some Evangelists
by Roger Carswell

Your church has a pastor and teachers – but where are your evangelists? Seek out who your evangelists are and send them out. Roger Carswell sets out the biblical focus on evangelism. Be prepared to be challenged. With a lifetime of experience Carswell gives a practical and challenging resource to help equip Christians – whether pastors or future evangelists.

ISBN: 978-1-78191-519-6

WHAT IS A CHRISTIAN?

ROGER CARSWELL

What is a Christian?
by Roger Carswell

Roger Carswell asks the question, "Why does it matter anyway?" The chapters are headed – A Christian has recognised who God is; A Christian has repented of wrong; A Christian has received what Jesus offers; A Christian is revelling in what they have.

Rogers writes, "This little volume is unpacking the distinctives that make Christian belief so vibrant and joyful. It attempts to unearth the core beliefs that Christians have in common."

ISBN: 978-1-78191-272-0

Christian Focus Publications

Our mission statement –

STAYING FAITHFUL
In dependence upon God we seek to impact the world through literature faithful to His infallible Word, the Bible. Our aim is to ensure that the Lord Jesus Christ is presented as the only hope to obtain forgiveness of sin, live a useful life and look forward to heaven with Him.

Our books are published in four imprints:

CHRISTIAN
FOCUS

Popular works including biographies, commentaries, basic doctrine and Christian living.

CHRISTIAN
HERITAGE

Books representing some of the best material from the rich heritage of the church.

MENTOR

Books written at a level suitable for Bible College and seminary students, pastors, and other serious readers. The imprint includes commentaries, doctrinal studies, examination of current issues and church history.

CF4•K

Children's books for quality Bible teaching and for all age groups: Sunday school curriculum, puzzle and activity books; personal and family devotional titles, biographies and inspirational stories – because you are never too young to know Jesus!

Christian Focus Publications Ltd,
Geanies House, Fearn, Ross-shire,
IV20 1TW, Scotland, United Kingdom.
www.christianfocus.com